Vocational Business

3

Marketing

Keith Brumfitt, Stephen Barnes, Liz Norris & Jane Jones

Series Editor: Keith Brumfitt

Published in 2001 by:
Nelson Thornes Ltd
Delta Place
27 Bath Road
CHELTENHAM
GL53 7TH
United Kingdom

01 02 03 04 05 / 10 9 8 7 6 5 4 3 2 1

A catalogue record for this book is available from the British Library

ISBN 0 7487 6361 9

Illustrations by Oxford Designers and Illustrators

Page make-up and illustrations by GreenGate Publishing Services, Tonbridge, Kent

Printed and bound in Italy by Stige

Contents

Introduction to Vocational Business series

This textbook is one of a series of six covering the core areas of business studies. Each book focuses on vocational aspects of business, rather than theoretical models, allowing the reader to understand how businesses operate. To complement this vocational focus, each book contains a range of case studies illustrating how businesses respond to internal and external changes.

The textbooks are designed to support students taking a range of business courses. While each is free standing, containing the essential knowledge required by the various syllabuses and course requirements, together they provide a comprehensive coverage of the issues facing both large and small businesses in today's competitive environment.

Titles in the series

Acknowledgements

The authors and publishers would like to thank the following people and organisations for permission to reproduce photographs and other material:

Arla Foods; Booker Cash & Carry; Cadbury Schweppes plc; First Direct; the Ford Motor Co.; Greenpeace UK; Mars UK Limited; Next Retail Ltd; Pearson Education Ltd; Sony UK Ltd; St Ivel Ltd; Tate & Lyle plc; Tesco; Waitrose Ltd; Yoplait-Dairy Crest/Toucan.

Every effort has been made to contact copyright holders, and we apologise if any have been overlooked.

Marketing

Introduction

Marketing is about understanding the customer and ensuring that products and services match existing and potential customers' needs. Marketing is also about looking at ways of influencing the behaviour of customers. In this book you will get inside the marketing process from carrying out initial research into a market to asking about the success or otherwise of a strategy. You will investigate the principles and functions of marketing and the way in which they contribute to generating income and/or profit in business.

Marketing involves matching customer needs and bringing products to customers' attention

How does marketing work?

What is marketing?

Anything you decide to sell needs bringing to the market. Sometimes this is simple. For example, you might take some vinyl records to a car-boot sale. But if you want to sell a bicycle, it may be necessary to advertise in a newsagent's window or in the local paper. Selling a house is usually more complicated. Most people place the sale in the hands of an estate agent, who will publicise the property and send details to a large number of possible purchasers.

Figure 3.1 Bringing the product to market

Marketing involves:

- **researching consumer needs and wants**

- **analysing the nature of the market to ensure a match between the firm's capabilities and the demand identified**

- **shaping the product to fit demand**

- **promoting the product to increase its value among potential customers**

- **distributing the product so that it is available in the right places at the right times**

- **setting a price for the product that ensures satisfaction for the customer and profitability for the firm.**

▶ Demand, page 9

There are also 'products' that are 'sold' in less obvious ways. For example, a charity may want to explain the importance of its cause to encourage the public to make donations. Or the government may want to stress to motorists the link between drinking alcohol and car accidents in order to reduce road casualties.

The effective presentation of a product in its target market is the essence of good marketing. The American marketing expert, Philip Kotler, says marketing can be briefly defined as 'meeting needs profitably'. The same idea is put more fully by the Institute of Marketing in Britain: 'Marketing is the management process involved in identifying, anticipating and satisfying consumer requirements profitably.'

For a business organisation, successful marketing achieves sales, generates profit and leaves the customer feeling fully satisfied. In today's increasingly competitive markets, no organisation can afford to neglect the quality of its marketing.

This was not always so. Before the industrial revolution, most business units were small and produced for the local community where the market was quite literally outside the door. Marketing as a specialised activity developed during the nineteenth and early twentieth centuries. Larger firms used machines to mass-produce goods and exploited improved communications to sell them in national and overseas markets. Today, marketing is often the driver of business activity. But what exactly does it involve?

We know that the job of combining resources to achieve the output of goods and services is called production. Correspondingly the purchase and use of those goods and services is called consumption. Marketing is everything that connects production with consumption.

Producers and consumers meet in the market place. Some towns still have traditional markets where sellers and buyers meet face to face. But most transactions today are made through retail shops or by direct sales media such as mail order, telephone or the Internet. In fact, a market is any medium through which buyers and sellers agree a price.

 Market research, page 12

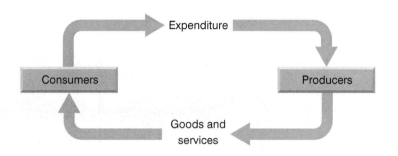

Expenditure

Consumers

Producers

Goods and services

Key term

Price is the amount of money or value agreed for a buyer to pay a seller in exchange for the product offered.

Figure 3.2 *Production/consumption as a two-way link*

CTIVITY

Suggest at least one good way of communicating with potential customers to sell each of the following products:

- jeans
- climbing holidays
- quality French wines
- a gardening service
- packing machines.

Assume in each case that, as a business person, you are selling to the final user of the product.

 Price, page 37

The idea of price deserves a closer look. Markets are really about swapping or exchanging. Marketing has two foundation elements: the product and the price. A sale involves exchanging money for a product.

Put another way, the consumer gives up money and gets a product while a producer gives up a product and gets money. Why? Logically we can assume that the consumer believes that they have got the best value for money and producers believe that they have got the best price for their product. And as with any swap, both sides feel better off. The consumer has the satisfaction of good value while the producer has a financial profit.

It follows that a key task of the marketing department in any organisation is to make its product more attractive relative to price. There is a risk that the effort to make a product more attractive will push up costs – and therefore price – to a level that is unacceptable. The basis of successful marketing is to make the product distinctively attractive while keeping its price acceptable to the target consumer – and still profitable for the business.

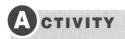

ACTIVITY

Figure 3.3 *Priced out of the market?*

Barlings was a busy restaurant which aimed to meet the needs of the local professional and business community for good quality meals. After a slight dip in takings caused by the opening of a competitor, the owners completed a customer survey to find out what they would most like from a restaurant. The result was a major upgrading with more luxurious furnishings and decor, a top quality chef and an exceptional wine cellar. Unfortunately, higher costs made it necessary to increase prices by just over 50 per cent. Within a few weeks the restaurant was almost empty as customers headed for less costly competitors. What had gone wrong?

Suppose you were asked by Barlings to suggest what had gone wrong. What would you say?

Product versus market orientation

Until the 1950s most firms tended to focus on the nature of their product rather than the needs of their market. In other words, they planned the output of their product and then looked for a market. Such a firm is said to be product oriented and many still exist. In practice it means that confidence is placed in a product (or range of products) which is often well established or familiar in its market. Customers are expected to buy the product because they always have done and because it is 'good'.

This approach carries great dangers. Consumer tastes are always changing and new technologies constantly develop. This is particularly true today. Meanwhile competitors are looking for ways of capturing new customers by offering better value.

CASE STUDY

Big Blue

The American company, IBM, is the world's largest producer of computers. It has always been famous for the quality of its technology and its powerful mainframe machines. But during the 1980s competitors reduced their prices while consumer demand switched to desktop computers. By 1993 the once-mighty IBM faced massive losses and was forced to cut jobs and begin the tough job of catching up with the market.

Want to know more?

Back in 1960 the American business writer Theodore Levitt published a famous article called 'Marketing Myopia'. In this he made a simple but very telling point. American railroads – which were losing customers to cars and roads – thought they were in the business of running trains. Wrong, said Levitt: their business was transport, meeting the needs of people for travel.

Starting with the market, with people and their needs, is called market orientation. It means buyers, not sellers, decide what should be produced and how it should be presented for sale.

 What's the demand?, page 9

CASE STUDY

BT

Until 1980, telephone services in Britain were owned and run by the Post Office. Telephones were only offered in a few unimaginative designs, to rent and not to buy. Getting a phoneline connected could take six weeks. The emphasis was on proper procedures and correct dialling.

The telephone service was privatised in 1987 and today BT is a customer-focused business. The communication needs of people, not telephones, are the market and BT is constantly watching for new needs and the new technologies through which they can be met.

It was exactly this approach that enabled so many Japanese companies to win command of the market for cameras, videos, hi-fi and other electrical goods. They studied in great detail what customers really

Consumer wants, page 12

wanted in a product and the price they were prepared to pay. Then exactly that product was manufactured with great efficiency and exported all over the world.

ACTIVITY

Figure 3.4 *The Headland Hotel*

The Headland Hotel offers traditional accommodation and stresses its comfortable lounges and sea-views. It has 50 rooms, two bars, a ballroom and formal restaurant.

Brainstorm at least three ways in which market orientation might change what is offered by the Headland Hotel.

Marketing involves a two-way transmission. This means:
- there is the effort to increase sales between producer and consumer
- the product and its promotion and distribution have to be at the right price
- a strong flow of information between consumer and producer
- detailed research into the wants of potential customers and the environment within which the firm operates.

Only by ensuring the consumer and the seller are properly linked can the organisation become market-oriented.

What about the competition?

When walking down today's high street, it is easy to feel that the big names have always been there and always will be there. This is an illusion. Many firms and brands that were household names in the 1960s and 70s are now dead and largely forgotten. No firm – no matter how famous – has a right to be in business.

Figure 3.5 *Well known – but for how long?*

CASE STUDY

Marks & Spencer

Until 1998 Marks & Spencer seemed to be a firm that was always winning. Year after year the company expanded in Britain and overseas. Sales, profits and share price appeared to defy gravity.

Then in late 1998 – without warning – progress faltered. The autumn fashion range appeared to have flopped. Sales and profits turned down. It was soon clear that this was not just a setback but the start of something more serious. The year 1999 brought no relief. Sales of clothing fell by more than 10 per cent as the downturn spread into home furnishings. Even food sales were suffering. Marks & Spencer was losing share to C&A, George of Asda, Next and Gap – to mention a few of its competitors.

What was wrong? Many commentators pointed to poor lighting, bad layout and uninspired product ranges. But Lisa Armstrong, fashion editor at The Times, argued that the problem has been a failure to understand the new lives of women who switch between roles in romance, motherhood and work in a fast-changing and complex pattern. Profits for 2000 were around £450 million, compared with well over £1,000 million two years earlier.

What can marketing achieve?

Marketing objectives

Before starting to explore the goals of marketing, we need to know what business organisations are aiming to achieve. What exactly is meant by business success? We know that there is no simple answer. Besides needing to meet the aims of shareholders, some firms have a range of other stakeholder interests that they wish to fulfil. None of these interests can be satisfied in the long term unless the firm makes a profit.

Increasing profitability

Profitability depends not only on making a profit but also on the level of profit relative to the size of the business. £1 million profit might be an exceptional performance for a family-owned hotel but a disaster for a national chain store. There are two broad approaches to achieving profitability.

One approach is to sell a large volume of the product on a fairly small margin of profit while the other is to sell a small volume at a high profit margin. For example, retailers selling groceries usually trade on a high volume but a small margin. Specialist jewellers, by contrast, accept lower volumes, but expect a higher margin. Each market is different but the need for profitability is the same.

Key terms

Profitability is the level of profit achieved by a business enterprise relative to its size. The level of profitability can vary widely over time and between businesses.

Profit margin is the percentage of sales value that is profit.

Although achieving and sustaining profitability will always be a long-term goal of any marketing plan, there can be a more immediate need for income or cash. An organisation may need to repay debts, or invest in new equipment, or expand through buying other business units. Sometimes managers may have to accept some reduction in profitability in order to raise enough cash.

Increasing market share

Some organisations set their goals in terms of the market. One objective that often runs alongside profitability is growth, which is usually measured in terms of market share.

$$\text{Market share} = \frac{\text{Sales of firm}}{\text{Total sales in given market}} \times 100$$

Market share can be measured in terms of value (sales in £) or volume (sales by quantity). Changes in a firm's sales can then be seen in context. For example, if the sales of a firm increase by 10 per cent, is this good performance? If the size of the total market has only grown by 5 per cent, then the firm's market share must now be larger. But if the same sales increase was set against a 20 per cent expansion in the total market, then the firm has actually lost ground in terms of market share.

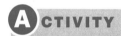CTIVITY

Tesco versus Sainsbury's

Table 3.1 *Market shares of UK grocery sales for Tesco and Sainsbury's from 1995–1999*

Year	Sainsbury's Sales £m	Market share %	Tesco Sales £m	Market share %
1996	13.5	15.1	12.1	13.9
1997	14.3	15.0	13.9	14.6
1998	15.5	14.3	16.5	14.7
1999	16.4	14.6	17.2	15.1
2000	17.4	14.6	18.8	15.3

Source: Company reports 1996–2000.

Suppose you were a financial manager at Sainsbury's.
1 Calculate the annual rate of growth in sales for your company and Tesco.
2 Compare your UK market share with the equivalent data for Tesco over the period 1996–2000.
3 Use a spreadsheet package to graph the data.
4 Comment carefully on the performance of your company relative to Tesco. What other data would you want to make a fuller assessment?

Firms may grow by taking over another firm in the same type of business. For example, in 1994 Tesco took over William Low, a Scottish supermarket chain. Alternatively there is always the possibility of growth through diversification. Some firms have the expertise to diversify for themselves (e.g. Virgin's decision to offer pensions) while others acquire another company in order to enter the new market (e.g. purchase of Kwik-Fit by Ford).

 Diversification, page 27

Can demand be satisfied?

CASE STUDY

Tesco

'Every little helps' is the slogan in Tesco's supermarkets. Less well known is the slogan in Tesco's Annual Report: 'Customer driven'. This continues: 'Responding to the customer is the core of Tesco's strategy.'

Figure 3.6 *Responding to the market*

The market-oriented organisation aims to respond to changes in customer needs or wants. If it falls behind its competitors in its ability to respond, either sales will fall or price cuts will be necessary, in both cases squeezing profits.

Anticipating changes in consumer needs can be as difficult as forecasting the weather. Tesco has millions of customers with individual needs. Somehow the firm must try to track the changing tastes and preferences of people according to age group, gender, geographical region and lifestyle. Like weather forecasters, managers continually survey conditions in many different places at once. In the course of this market research they make extensive use of information technology to collect and analyse results which then feed into pricing and marketing decisions.

It is not just a matter of keeping pace with customer needs. For a real competitive edge, firms need to be ahead of the game, actually *anticipating* needs that have often barely emerged. This means learning to identify patterns and trends as well as making 'jumps' in product offering or customer service that catch competitors unawares and increase market share. As in all business initiatives, there is risk and uncertainty. Yet sometimes there is greater risk in failing to act.

Key term

Market research entails collecting and analysing information about the behaviour and preferences of consumers.

Figure 3.7

St Ivel

St Ivel seeks to extend and revitalise its brands continually through new products, packaging, additional flavours and imaginative advertising and promotional strategies.

The 'Utterly Butterly' spread combined the taste and texture of butter and turned St Ivel into the second largest manufacturer of spreads in Britain. In 1999 and 2000 St Ivel extended its successful range of Cadbury's desserts to include Flake and Caramel Dessert, relaunched and repackaged the Shape range of yoghurts and Fromage Frais and introduced spreadable cheese pots and the popular pick 'n' mix cheeses. To stay ahead, the market-driven firm must be 'lean and hungry' for change. It must also be nimble and quick in spotting market opportunity. As American writer Tom Peters says: 'Tomorrow's successful corporation will be a collection of skills and capabilities ever ready to pounce on brief market opportunities.'

Opportunities are created by change, and gaps in the market can appear quite suddenly. Winning firms will be those quickest to recognise a widening gap in the market and to fill it with an outstanding product.

A CTIVITY

Reinventing pen and paper

Some of the best ideas are obvious once someone has thought of them e.g. the mobile phone or Post-it notes. Everyone knows that technology can be used to develop existing products and services, but would you have thought of creating a new pen and paper? Anoto, a new technology company, has.

The new pen includes a digital camera, which records everything you write. This information is processed and transmitted to a computer via an Internet phone. This creates amazing possibilities. You could write a card at any Interflora shop and the recipient of the flowers could receive an identical copy of the note you wrote on the card as it could be downloaded from the receiving computer. Salespeople could complete order forms or book appointments and the information could be automatically sent to their computers at work. Solicitors and others could keep a record of everything they write, thereby avoiding the need for photocopies and the typing of notes.

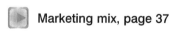
Marketing mix, page 37

Tasks

1 Can you identify five uses of this type of pen?
2 Can you identify potential customers for the pen?
3 Devise a marketing strategy for one of these groups of potential customers – this should include the four aspects of the marketing mix.

Keeping the customer satisfied?

Whatever else is done by a marketing department, keeping the customer satisfied is the top priority. Customers who are not satisfied will reduce the quantity of the product they purchase or will switch to a competitor for supply. The old saying that in business 'the customer is always right' reflects the importance of ensuring that customers' needs and expectations are fully met. In most organisations the 1990s saw an increased emphasis on quality in every area of operations. Competition can be seen as external pressure to keep up continual improvement in quality.

This clearly means quality in the product, whether services or manufactured goods. But it also means quality in advertising or sales promotion, customer service and after-sales support. Customers form a lasting impression of a product or brand through their total experience of the firm. Loyal customers are hard to win but easy to lose. It follows that reputation is a vital asset for successful organisations. The reputation for everyday quality enjoyed by Boots or British Airways is extremely powerful in building and protecting their market share and in achieving long-term profitability.

CASE STUDY

Figure 3.8 A reputation for quality: Marks & Spencer Financial Services centre

When introduced in 1985, the Marks & Spencer charge card was seen as just another big store credit system. However, by 2000 Marks & Spencer was the third largest provider of financial services in the non-bank sector. In other words it had become a major player in a business that was not traditionally its own. Through electronic data recording the card is also a major source of market information and customer loyalty.

Brands, page 46

Often an organisation's reputation for delivering customer satisfaction becomes concentrated in its name, its brand or even its logo.

This favourable perception by consumers is usually built by management over a long period. Under an 'umbrella' of reputation, new products have an increased chance of success while consumers are often willing to pay a premium price for the right 'name'. Reputation and a strong brand also greatly assist diversification and entry into new markets.

 ## CASE STUDY

Until the 1970s the brand name of 'Virgin' was only associated with records. No one anticipated the company's successful entry into the markets for air travel, soft drinks or pensions. But the Virgin brand became a force in its own right. An image that spoke of youth, energy, efficiency – even breaking the rules – all played in Virgin's favour. The strength of the brand grew to such an extent that it could cross product boundaries and win market share from a standing start.

| Market research

What is market research?

We have seen that business involves bringing to the market products that people want. Provided that the cost of all input to a product is exceeded by the price, then a profit can be achieved. But this simple reasoning raises a range of questions:

- What is the market?
- Who are the customers?
- Where are the customers located?
- What exactly do people want?
- Which people?
- How many people?
- How keen are they to buy the product?
- What is the 'right' price?
- Suppose that the price was lower? Or higher?
- Can other firms offer the same product?
- How do competitors compare on cost? And price?
- What is the direction of change?
- What forces are acting on the market?
- Would these answers still be valid in a year's time?

Market research is the process of asking and answering questions of this kind. It began as an occasional effort by companies to know their customers better and turned into a worldwide multi-billion pound industry. Small firms – and particularly business start-ups – often carry out their own informal market research. This may simply mean talking to actual or potential customers or checking the prices charged by competitors. The effectiveness of informal research is likely to depend on the entrepreneur's willingness to 'listen' – to take customers and competitors seriously and always to be self-critical.

For larger firms, less can be left to chance. Professional market research uses scientific approaches and is likely to employ a specialised agency. This kind of contracting out takes place because market research is not in itself the firm's area of expertise. Its resources are usually better directed towards its core business activity.

Sometimes market research is directed to answering a specific one-off question. For example, should Burger King open a branch in a particular town? More often it is concerned with supplying a steady stream of information that can guide marketing decisions.

A business may need market research that is:

- tactical – shorter term and more detailed; for example, a restaurant may want to know the proportion of customers wanting a salad during the summer months
- strategic – longer term and larger in scale; for example, how is the average age of our customers at fast-food outlets changing?

Marketing Information Systems (MIS)

Firms must respond very quickly to changes in the marketing environment; otherwise their competitors will get there first. It is therefore not enough just to carry out market research when a problem arises. Instead a regular flow of marketing information needs to reach key managers in the right form at the right time. Many major firms around the world now operate a carefully constructed MIS.

An MIS collects, analyses and distributes information from:

- internal company data
- external intelligence
- market research.

Market information could be in two forms.

- **Quantitative data expresses exact amounts for any variable. For example, your sports centre may find out how many people use each of its facilities during each hour of opening.**

- **Qualitative data is information about people's judgements or feelings. For example, the sports centre might investigate how friendly users find its staff or how people judge its publicity.**

Want to know more?

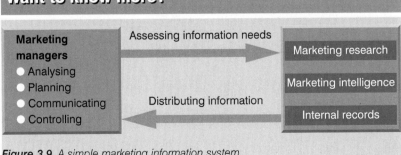

Figure 3.9 A simple marketing information system

Internal company data comes typically from finance and accounting, sales, customer service and production departments. Increasingly for retail firms, computerised loyalty card schemes (e.g. Tesco Clubcard) are greatly accelerating the flow of useful information about customers and their buying behaviour.

External intelligence captures information in the marketing environment. It can be collected from any department and by staff at any level. Sales and customer service are particularly important sources. Much depends on getting all staff to feel motivated in feeding back information. Intelligence also comes from publications (e.g. Annual Reports and Accounts) and can be purchased from specialist research organisations (e.g. AG Neilsen's retail surveys).

Market research is the gathering and analysing of information about the actual and potential demand for products in a marketplace. This process can provide a continuous flow of research information but is also a vital tool for investigating a particular problem or opportunity; e.g. should an ice-cream manufacturer launch a grapefruit-flavoured ice lolly?

Targeting market research

Every day we all contribute to the statistics of market research. Our consumption of most products is recorded somewhere and, through information technology, is increasingly linked to our address and even our identity.

CASE STUDY

TWIX

Figure 3.10 *TWIX (® TWIX is a registered trademark. Used by permission of Mars UK Limited)*

Market researchers will need to know answers to the following questions, to help them design their marketing campaigns.
- How are UK sales of TWIX changing?
- How well does TWIX sell in each UK region?
- What type of customers are the most frequent purchasers of TWIX?
- In what circumstances is TWIX most widely eaten?
- Which product is the closest competitor to TWIX?
- What kind of complaints are received about TWIX?

Every business has a goldmine of information about itself and its products. This includes:
- sales records by country/region/area and sometimes by customer
- the effectiveness of different distribution channels (e.g. chain stores or independent retailers)
- production volumes and values
- stock levels
- cost patterns.

Less precise but still valuable will be evidence from the salesforce about customer attitudes, competition, complaints and product problems. Computer technology has made the collection of internal information much faster, more reliable and far cheaper. Collation and analysis is often instantaneous by using a customised database.

However, there is a real risk of producing too much information that is poorly related to decision-making and wasteful of resources. Excessive flows of information (called information overload) can be a consequence of cheap computer-based data systems. Often one page of carefully selected key information is more valuable than hundreds of pages of unfocused or undigested material.

Market research is most effective when targeted with a clear purpose. Where it is task directed, the starting point is to get the firm's problem or opportunity into sharp focus. What information is needed? How will it help? To what extent? The answers to these questions need translating into cost-effective research. Then the actual collection, break-down and interpretation of data can take place. Finally the conclusions and supporting evidence must be communicated to the right people in the organisation. (See Figure 3.11.)

Marketing managers will not be able to find out *everything* about customers and markets that they would ideally like to know. It is simply too expensive – and time-consuming. Decisions must be made about the value of data relative to its cost. As a principle, the value of information must be greater than the opportunity cost of the resources required in its research. But managers will also have to keep within their budget for marketing expenses.

Key term

The **opportunity cost** of any decision is the value of the next best alternative.

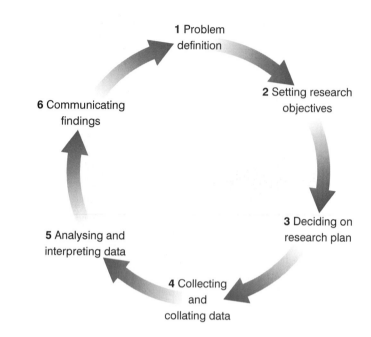

Figure 3.11 *The market research cycle*

Competitive advantage, page 22

Types of market research

The type of market research carried out depends on its purpose. For example, Perrier mineral water might carry out:

- exploratory research (sometimes called market intelligence) to help identify a problem or opportunity; for example, how is the UK soft drinks market changing?
- descriptive research to provide information about customers and their behaviour; for example, how are sales of Perrier split between age groups and socio-economic groups?
- experimental research to investigate possible causes and connections between variables; for example, how far does the bottle shape give Perrier a source of competitive advantage?

Market research methods

Primary research

The direct collection of original data from the marketplace is called primary research. It is also called 'field research' as it takes place 'in the field', i.e. in contact with the people and places concerned. By definition this is data that cannot be looked up in books or on databases. Its collection is designed to address a particular brief or specification. Although it can be very useful, primary research tends to be slow and expensive.

Secondary research

The use of information that is already available – at a cost or free – is called secondary or 'desk' research. It has not been collected for the firm's specific purpose but may throw light on the interesting issues. Secondary data may be internal (drawn from the firm's records) or it can be external and extracted from published material. Generally the use of secondary sources is cheaper and quicker than primary research.

Collecting primary data

Figure 3.12 Collecting primary data

Surveys are the main method used for collecting primary data. These are usually framed in the form of a questionnaire. There are three main methods of carrying out a survey:
- personal interviews
  - individual
  - group
- telephone interviews
- mail questionnaires.

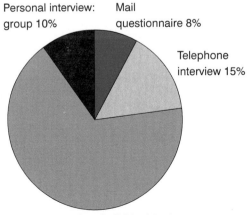

Figure 3.13 UK expenditure on primary data collection methods (Source: *Kotler* et al, Principles of Marketing (Prentice Hall, 1996))

17

ⒶCTIVITY

EMAP plc is a highly successful publisher of magazines and local newspapers. The mass circulation magazine market is fast-changing and strongly competitive. Innovation is vital to marketing at EMAP and ideas for new titles are under constant consideration. But to be realistic, any new magazine concepts need a carefully targeted readership.

Suppose that you are evaluating a possible new title *Inside TV*. The magazine would explore the world of TV programme-making and personalities with an emphasis on the family and non-specialist market. The core readership (regular buyers and readers who have a loyalty to the title) is likely to be women aged 25–45.

Tasks

1 How would you find out the type of features most likely to be popular with the target market?
2 How would you research the present and likely future size of your core readership?
3 If the magazine is launched, by what means might readers' satisfaction with early issues be assessed?
4 Why do new magazine titles often fail even after careful market research?

Personal interviews

A researcher talks to an individual or a group to find out more about consumer preferences or buying behaviour. For example, a firm developing a new soft drink may want to find out more about the preferences of people aged 16–25.

- Which flavourings are preferred?
- What are the most popular styles of packaging?
- What kind of image is most likely to appeal?

Individual interviews are usually carried out using questionnaires in the street or shopping centres or in private homes. Most interviews are fairly short and tend to rely on closed questions. Interviewees may be given a modest reward for their co-operation.

Personal interviews can be effective for most kinds of survey. Trained interviewers can assist and probe in collecting answers while respondents can be shown examples of products, packaging or publicity. But interviews are expensive and prone to unintended bias.

Panel discussions

These are a kind of group interview and involve a small number of people being invited to gather at an office suite or hotel to discuss a product or brand, e.g. soft drinks already on the market. A leader or moderator develops a relaxed atmosphere and gradually focuses the discussion on the target areas of interest. Later the session can be analysed through notes or video.

Telephone interviews

These are a quick and convenient way to apply a short questionnaire. Often it means cold-calling (contacting unknown respondents) but firms also use lists of existing or past customers. Although the response rate (proportion of people co-operating) is often fairly high, the method is quite costly and the interviewer's style may distort the answers.

Mail questionnaires

These have the advantage of being cheap and easy to target, e.g. sending a questionnaire to every customer of the past three years. The questions must be especially simple and clear since there is no help available from an interviewer. Unfortunately the response rate is usually very low.

 **CTIVITY**

THE WASHING POWDER WITH A WHITER WASH...

Figure 3.14

Suppose you were working at a marketing agency and were asked to comment on this questionnaire on 'Zenith' washing powder:

- How much do you earn?
- Do you agree that Zenith gives a whiter wash?
- How many kilos of washing powder did you buy last year?
- Does it matter to you that clothes are really clean and fragrant?
- Is it important that the price of detergent should be low?
- Are you against the use of artificial chemicals in washing powders?
- Which brand of powder were you using five years ago?
- To what extent do you accept the hypothesis that Zenith is a superior product?

Tasks

1 Make a brief criticism of each each question.
2 Suggest a better set of questions.

Questionnaires
A good questionnaire depends on clear objectives for the research. These are then expressed through a series of carefully constructed questions. The format for answers can be designed for easy analysis, often by computer. The purpose of the questionnaire should be made clear except when this needs to be disguised. For example, the owner of a betting shop may ask, 'Do you regularly try to pick winners?' rather than 'Do you place bets regularly?' Key guidelines for constructing an effective questionnaire are:

- make clear the purpose of the questionnaire (unless using a disguised approach)
- arrange questions in a logical order
- use clear, unambiguous language
- never ask intrusive personal questions
- keep down the total number of questions
- exclude biased or leading questions
- avoid depending too much on memory.

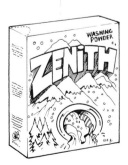

Sampling

If cost and time were unimportant, a firm might interview every possible customer in the UK. The realistic alternative is to consult a representative sample of the relevant population (all the people eligible for inclusion in the survey). Clearly sampling means that 100 per cent accuracy is not possible. The larger the sample size, the greater the accuracy but the greater the cost. Fortunately, as sample size increases, the level of accuracy rises very rapidly: even for very large populations a sample size of 2,000 is acceptably accurate. This is how opinion polls can use quite small samples to predict the views of millions of people.

There are several different ways in which samples can be drawn from a given population.

Random sampling

A random sample means that every member of a given population has an equal chance of being selected. This sounds easy to achieve but simply standing in a High Street at 11 a.m. will result in a very biased sample, i.e. few employed people will be selected while far too many non-working and retired people will be included.

Stratified sampling

A stratified sample means that respondents are selected from one or more identifiable groups in a population. For example, 40 per cent of the sample might be female including 10 per cent who are under 18.

Quota sampling

A quota sample makes the use of a stratified sampling approach more practicable. The total size of the intended sample is split proportionally between the various categories identified for the stratified sample. The researcher then consults exactly enough respondents to fill the 'quota' for each category.

CASE STUDY

Sounds Unlikely

The editorial team of this popular music paper want to introduce some new features but need to know more about their readers' listening habits. A market research agency is told that 80 per cent of its readership is aged 15–25 and 75 per cent is male. An appropriate questionnaire is prepared. How could respondents be selected?

Clearly a stratified sample which reflects the age and gender break-down of readers should be used. Quota sampling will make this process more practicable. The number of respondents to be consulted can be made proportional to their importance in the readership population.

The agency decides to carry out 1,000 interviews. Of these a quota of 600 interviews will be with young men aged 15–25 (80 per cent 15–25 = 800; 75 per cent male = 600). Another quota would be for women aged 15–25 and others for people under 15 or over 25.

Cluster sampling

Cluster sampling involves identifying and surveying a comparatively small population as representative of the whole population. For example, a firm making fitted kitchens might interview every household on one new estate which they consider to be representative of their overall market. This is clearly more efficient but any error in the selection of the cluster could cause serious bias in the results.

Obtaining secondary data

Huge amounts of useful data are openly available without charge. The Internet has become an almost infinitely large source of secondary data though the quality of websites is very variable. However, expert use of the Internet can find very valuable and up-to-date information. Equally a visit to a good public or university library can yield masses of information which is increasingly available on CD-ROM: official statistics, government reports, specialist books, journals, newspapers and more. Useful information about competitors can be found in annual reports and data filed at Companies House. Many other private sector organisations will supply outsiders with detailed information about their activities. Incomplete pictures can often be resolved by combining fragments of data from different sources.

Because it is valuable, there is a large market in secondary data. For example, AG Neilsen (a subsidiary of Dun & Bradstreet, the world's largest research organisation) is famous for retail audits and its Scantrack service supplies detailed information on competitors' prices and market shares of major stores. Vast amounts of usefully grouped and collated secondary data are available on-line from a range of agencies operating on a worldwide basis.

In addition, internal data, such as the transactions that contributed to the final accounts, provides valuable information. The published results of companies are only the barest summary of the events that they reflect. Thousands – often millions – of transactions have contributed to a set of accounts. These can all be analysed. When added to qualitative data, such as customers' comments, a much better insight into a problem can be achieved.

Marketing strategies

What is a competitive advantage?

CASE STUDY

Perfect competition

The organisers of a village fete offer local students the chance to sell soft drinks from stalls on the village green. Three small groups of students take their chance. On the Friday before the fete they all visit the local cash-and-carry and buy crates of Coke. The price per can works out at 24p.

The following afternoon sees three stalls offering cans of Coke. Rob's stall is charging 40p while Louise and friends aim higher at 50p. They are both surprised to see Nick's group scribbling out a new sign offering cans at 35p. A queue quickly forms around Nick's stall. Rob and Louise have no customers.

Ten minutes later Louise has slashed her price to 32p and attracted Nick's queue straight to her own table. Then Rob cuts his price to 30p and the punters are over to him. Not to be outdone, Nick hoists another sign: 'Rock bottom price. Coke at 29p'. The others groan. 'It's barely worth being here at 5p profit.'

After another ten minutes there are three stalls, each with a short queue and each charging 29p.

This situation is called perfect competition because there is nothing to get in the way of the competitive process. Buyers can see everything and sellers have nowhere to hide! Firms make just enough to stay in business but no more.

How can a firm do better? The answer lies in doing something better or different as compared with the other firms. Suppose that in the above example Nick had found a cash-and-carry where Coke was only 23p per can. Then he could charge 29p and still make 6p profit – 1p more than the 5p profit made by everyone else. Alternatively, suppose that Louise got buckets of ice and chilled her cans first. She might then charge 30p and still attract customers who are willing to pay extra for a more refreshing drink. Once again the profit per can is now 6p. This new situation is called imperfect competition – not because it is really 'imperfect' but because the conditions affecting buyers and sellers are no longer exactly equal.

In the real business world all firms aim to make a higher profit. This is often possible because they compete 'imperfectly'. Production costs vary from firm to firm while similar products are made to seem different.

Look back to the village fete when each stall competed on identical terms. Put another way, the stalls were competitively equal: no one stall had any competitive advantage over another. Then think about Nick's cheaper cash-and-carry and Louise's idea for chilling the cans. In each case the stall gained a competitive advantage and began to earn higher profit.

Some sources of competitive advantage are quickly lost as competitors copy one another. If Nick can find a cheaper cash-and-carry, then the others will do the same. Similarly, if chilling the cans costs nothing then the other stalls will chill theirs and price will fall back to 29p. But suppose Rob's stall has a great stock of jokes and decides to make buying Coke at the fete more fun by offering a 'free joke with every can'. He might now be able to charge 30p for the rest of the day, still attract customers and be safe from imitation.

How does competitive advantage work?

Exactly the same principle explains the competitive success of many businesses. The theory of competitive advantage was developed in the United States by Igor Ansoff and Michael Porter (*Competitive Strategy*, Michael Porter (Free Press, 1980)) who found that there were three possible routes by which firms might achieve a sustainable competitive advantage:

1 cost leadership
2 differentiation
3 focus.

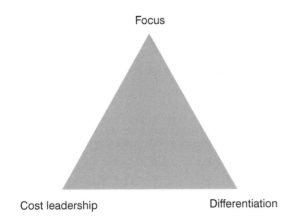

Figure 3.15 *Competitive advantage*

Cost leadership

This involves creating the lowest cost structure in the industry. Once achieved, the firm can pass on part of the benefit to customers in the form of lower prices. This can allow a large market share which may make it possible to cut costs even further.

Brands, page 46

CASE STUDY

Asda

Asda – now part of the US Wal-Mart group – is a fast-growing food and household goods chain. There are currently 240 Asda supermarkets in Britain based on the principle of offering the consumer the best possible value through low prices. The style of marketing is mostly cheap and cheerful: keeping down costs and prices is the key to business success.

Differentiation

This means selling products that are different from those of rivals and being able to offer the customer greater overall benefit. Such products can be sold at a premium price, i.e. a price that is higher than that charged by competitors.

Differentiation takes many forms. It may be as simple as offering colours or flavours that others do not. It can involve special technical features or touches of extra luxury. Sometimes it is as simple as the quality of customer service. Often, it is based on the image or reputation of a brand.

Want to know more?

Market segments are sections of a market as defined by a yardstick such as age-group, socio-economic group or specialist interest. Market segmentation is the process of dividing a market into segments which may then be targeted through the marketing mix.

Figure 3.16 Waitrose

CASE STUDY

Waitrose is the food-retailing arm of the John Lewis Partnership. It is an expanding chain of 136 supermarkets located mainly in traditional town centres across the south of England. The stores are positioned several notches up-market from Sainsbury's or Tesco with an emphasis on fresh foods and luxury products. Some prices can be above those at other supermarkets and few customers would say that price was their only priority. Significantly, margins are strong and sales are growing.

Focus

The business focuses on a fairly narrow section of the market and the marketing strategy is directed at the needs of these particular customers. As other firms try to achieve cost leadership or general differentiation, the firm with focus enjoys a competitive advantage in serving its own customers.

Within the strategy of focus, the firm may aim for cost leadership or differentiation.

CASE STUDY

Figure 3.17 *Taste of Italy*

Based in a prosperous commuter town outside London, Taste of Italy has three branches each offering specialist Italian foods. The company imports fresh pasta, fruit juices, cheeses, hams and other goods in addition to baking its own range of Italian bread. Prices are slightly above supermarket levels but the products are distinctive and the presentation is excellent.

Michael Porter argued that focus apart, firms should choose between cost leadership and differentiation. Trying to have the best of both worlds (i.e. low prices and differentiated products) would lead to being 'stuck-in-the-middle' with lower profitability.

Strategic directions

Almost no firm can stand still. Marketing decisions lead a firm in a particular direction. This can be called 'strategic' when it represents a longer-term trend that involves a significant part of the firm's resources.

The idea of strategic direction was first analysed by Ansoff back in the 1960s (Igor Ansoff, *Corporate Strategy* (McGraw Hill, 1965)). He identified two key factors: the market and the product. For each of these two factors the firm has a choice: no change or change. This gives rise to a simple grid:

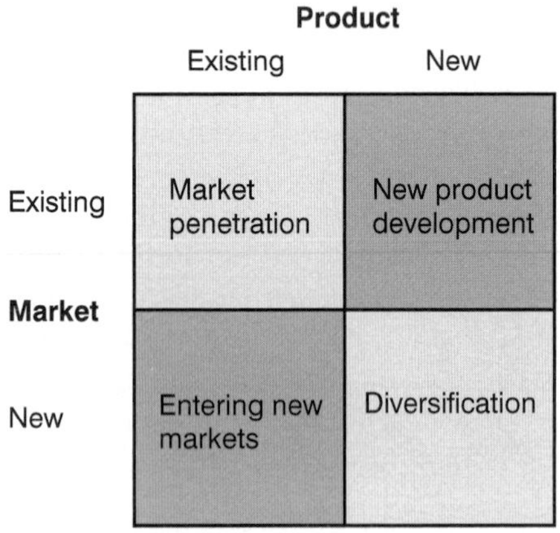

	Product	
	Existing	New
Market Existing	Market penetration	New product development
New	Entering new markets	Diversification

Figure 3.18 Ansoff matrix

Market penetration

This means taking an increasing share of the existing market with the same basic product. A firm may develop a cost advantage to offer lower prices than those of competitors. Equally it may improve product quality or variety of styles. It can also increase its marketing expenditure, e.g. on advertising.

There are other interpretations of 'existing market, existing product'. In some cases a firm may only want to consolidate or secure its position in the market. This is unlikely to involve no action at all. Pressure from competitors could involve cutting the cost base or improving quality.

Market oriented, page 4

New Product Development (NPD)

Products do not remain successful in the market for ever. The way people live changes, fashions come and go, new technologies emerge. Today there is more pressure than ever on firms to be effective in new product development and to seize market opportunities.

Successful NPD can bring huge rewards but it is costly and prone to failure. Few new product ideas survive the screening and testing phases and among products actually launched there is a high rate of failure. Prospects are improved by careful market research and a strong focus on the wants of target customers throughout the development process.

Entering new markets

This strategy aims to take an existing product into new market segments or new markets. As the pattern and character of market segments change continuously new opportunities may open up in a new geographical region or in another country. Perhaps the product will succeed with an older or younger age group or through a different distribution chain. This may require repackaging with changes in its image or market identity.

Diversification

In Ansoff's model this means both marketing a new product and entering a new market. Related diversification involves breaking out of existing product and market boundaries but retaining a common theme to the firm's overall pattern of business activity. For example, Virgin has diversified from its origins in recorded music to embrace air travel, soft drinks, insurance, banking, railways and more. But these are all leisure-related or service industries where a strong brand is important.

By contrast, unrelated diversification entails starting or buying businesses that are entirely different. A firm made up of unrelated business activities is called a conglomerate. Often the only links between the business units are the skills of management or financial control.

 **ASE STUDY**

Tomkins plc

Conglomerates have been out of fashion but Greg Hutchings of Tomkins plc built a vast business empire based on diversification. The company began in 1982 as a manufacturer of industrial fastenings with sales worth £25 million. By 1990, with sales soaring to £1 billion, Tomkins had entered dozens of industrial goods markets with major operations in the United States – including ownership of Smith & Wesson, world famous for guns and handcuffs.

In 1993 Hutchings won control of the British foods group, Rank-Hovis-McDougal, making his company the owner of the second largest milling and bread-making operation in the UK plus a long list of consumer brands such as Mr Kipling, Golden Shred and Just Juice.

But 'guns and cakes' proved an uncomfortable combination. Despite some success in cutting costs and improving profitability, the Rank-Hovis-McDougal operation was sold in 2000. In the same year Hutchings resigned and for a while in 2001 the firm seriously considered its own break-up.

Figure 3.19 Guns and cakes

A firm's basic choice of direction in marketing strategy is decided by top management, and its future success – even its very survival – depends on the right decisions.

Ansoff's matrix provides a number of directions for the firm's future development. Any choice must be based on the firm's core competences, in other words 'what it's good at'.

The advice of the American writer Tom Peters (1982) was 'stick to the knitting' or keep to what the business is 'all about'. There is always a danger of making products or entering markets that do not match up with any special talent in the firm. For instance, should the professional golfer who owns The Golf Shop start selling clothing and accessories for tennis? If enthusiasm for golf is the heart of the business, then the answer is probably 'No'. Once again, competitive advantage is a key concept. No plan for the expansion of a business is likely to succeed unless it is based on a sustainable source of competitive advantage. 'What makes us special?' is a very important question for managers.

Product evaluation

Managing products

A firm does not raise revenue but it does incur costs: only its products can generate revenue. Ultimately a firm's products are its life support system. They must fight for their existence in the marketplace and earn the profits necessary to fund the next generation of products that will replace them.

It follows that marketing managers must keep all products under constant review. Like members of a professional football team, products must score goals, contribute to overall strategy and expect close analysis of their form. But unlike football, the business game keeps changing. A product may continue to dominate a market segment but if that same segment is shrinking, then a winner can still become a loser.

CASE STUDY

A zest for lemon?

When Nestlé took over Rowntree, it looked for some extra sparkle in its famous brands. Polos was a classic brand with a very strong identity yet only available as peppermints or fruit-flavoured boiled sweets. In 1991 lemon Polos were test-marketed through major channels in the confectionery trade. Despite a good initial response, sales failed to reach their target. Two years later spearmint Polos proved a winner and as a successful extension of the Polo brand they have performed well ever since. Ironically, the lemon Polos concept was relaunched in 1998 as Citrus Sharp and this time sales took off.

New product development

The products that we see in the shops are winners. They may not all be profitable and some may not survive very long, but they are winners just to be there. Typically around twenty serious product ideas might be necessary to yield one product with enough promise to be launched. However, once launched the failure rate is still severe: perhaps around two thirds of consumer products and one third of industrial products fail within two years of their launch.

The most risky and expensive venture for a firm is the development of a new product. Yet only by innovating can most firms remain successful in a fast-changing marketplace. The more innovative the product, the greater the potential pay-off but the greater the cost and consequences of failure. The main types of new products are as follows.

- **Variant products** – these are fairly low-risk developments that are variations on an existing product. A machine might be given new features, a food product might be offered in new flavours or a holiday might be repackaged to include two resorts.
- **Imitative or 'Me-too' products** – when a truly innovative product becomes a winner, it always spawns a series of 'me-too' products which copy the original with a variety of small variations. The first product in a new field usually gains in reputation and market share but sometimes the 'me-toos' ride successfully on its back and gain a dominant share. Small firms that innovate are especially at risk from larger rivals with much greater marketing budgets.
- **Diversification products** – these are the products of a firm that breaks out of its traditional market and uses its experience and skills to enter new market territory. For example, a manufacturer of calculators might decide to launch an electronic game.
- **Innovative products** – least common but with most potential impact on the market are the real innovations. Some are fairly minor such as a new chocolate bar but others create whole new market sectors. Pentel's introduction of the first rollerball pen in 1976 and Mars' launch of their ice-cream bar in 1989 are examples. However, major innovations frequently fail and usually depend on the resources of a large firm.

Everyone is used to seeing the word 'New!' blazoned across products and shop windows. Very few people know about the months or even years of testing and planning that come before the launch of a new product.

Developing a new product begins with the generation of ideas, some of which are gathered from customers, suppliers and competitors. Large firms may have a formal R&D (Research and Development) department to initiate and experiment with product concepts.

Many firms use brainstorming sessions among managers to improve and extend their product range. Some businesses have a 'culture of innovation' where staff are always supported and encouraged in creative thinking.

> **Key term**
>
> **Product concept** means a basic outline of what a possible future product and its marketing might involve.

> **Key term**
>
> A **culture of innovation** means an atmosphere or 'way of doing things' within a firm that encourages questions, new thinking and new ideas.

ⓒASE STUDY

The fun Ka

Figure 3.20 Ford Ka

Ford is best known as an economical, good quality, mid-market company which sells family cars. The Ford brand is not widely associated with highly innovative, fashionable or exciting models.

The Ka was different. The idea began back in 1993 with the recognition that there was increasing demand in the small car market for economy with style. With an increasing number of women purchasers, Ford needed a vehicle that would cross the 'gender divide'.

Although the new product was to be very much a 'Ford', it was also conceived as a highly innovative car, radically different from its competitors, for example the Vauxhall Nova or the Fiat Uno. It would be extremely practical but fun to own and drive. The spirit of older but innovative classic small cars would not be far away: Citroen's 2CV, VW's Beetle, the Morris Minor and the Mini.

This product concept was highly rated against Ford's own criteria for product development. It was also liked in concept testing with representative consumers. The business analysis was also positive. The new product would extend the Ford range 'below' the best-selling Fiesta while being strongly differentiated from its competitors.

The projected vehicle gained its fuller identity in product development. The name – with its subtle play on letters and words – was a masterstroke. The Ford Ka would have all the utility and reliability of a Japanese competitor and yet the style and excitement of a quality European product.

The decision to produce the Ka was taken in 1994 and it was launched in late 1996 to an excellent reception from dealers and customers alike.

The product life cycle

Like people, products pass through a recognisable series of stages in their active lives. The phenomenon of a product life cycle was first described in the 1960s and has become an important tool of product and market analysis. The four phases most commonly identified are:

- introduction – the early days of slow sales growth after the product's launch
- growth – the take-off in sales as the product gains in popularity
- maturity – a period of high but fairly flat sales as the product enjoys its 'heyday'
- decline – a downward trend in sales as the product loses ground in the market.

The classic sales and profit curve represented by these stages is shown in Figure 3.21.

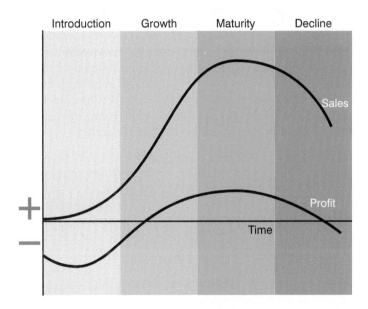

Figure 3.21 *The product life cycle*

It is important to recognise the distinction between sales and profit. By definition, profit is only ever a proportion of sales but it is a fraction which varies significantly across the different stages of the product life cycle.

For the marketing manager each stage of the life cycle has its own characteristics.

- The introduction stage begins the day the product is launched. After any initial surge of interest, the volume of sales is likely to grow only slowly at first. Marketing efforts are designed for innovative, opinion-forming consumers (people who like 'to try things'). Relatively high promotion and advertising expenditure will usually mean negative profits. If any competition exists it is likely to be limited. Price can be fairly high to recover development costs or lower to encourage first-time users.

- The growth stage sees a rapid acceleration in sales as the product is accepted in more segments of the market. Profit begins to be positive as costs are spread over higher sales volumes. Competitors may begin to enter an attractive market with 'me-too' variants of the original.
- The maturity stage is signalled by a levelling out of sales growth as the market becomes saturated. Competition is often intense and the firm has to use persuasive advertising to hold consumer loyalty. The marketing will emphasise the product being 'the original' and any special features. Product variants are often introduced at this stage in an effort to maintain consumer interest and to reach smaller segments. Profitability may begin to fall as competition drives down prices and discounting becomes important in the marketing mix.
- The decline stage sees falling sales as profits fade or disappear. Increasingly competitors drop out of the market. Marketing expenditure is reduced and price may be cut further. Before decline progresses far, the firm needs to decide on the product's future. One option is to relaunch the product through an extension strategy. This may only mean repackaging and a new promotion push or it may be more significant through a technical improvement or new product use. The alternative is to cut all marketing costs to a minimum and let the product decline while it can still earn some profits. Sooner or later it will be dropped altogether.

CASE STUDY

Sony

Figure 3.22 Sony: The real thing?

The life cycle for floppy disks has been running for about twenty years. It is currently in the maturity phase where it remains until threatened by a new technology. Since all disks are very similar in performance, individual producers need to find ways of differentiating their products. This can help retain market share and justify the price premium of a well known brand. A recent box design for Sony floppy disks states in a bold yellow flash: 'The 3.5" MFD was invented in 1980 by Sony.'

Coca-Cola
For many years Coca-Cola used the slogan: 'Coke: The Real Thing'. A clear warning that Pepsi is just an imitation.

Although products move through the stages at very different speeds, they all have a life cycle. However, the tighter the definition of the product, the shorter and more distinct its life cycle becomes. For example, Wall's Solero will be subject to a definite life cycle while ice lollies in general may enjoy fairly indefinite popularity.

The profile of the product life cycle varies widely among products.

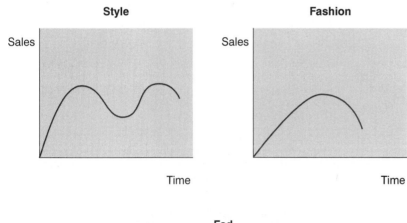

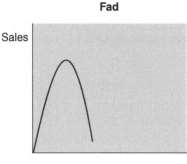

(*Source: Philip Kotler et al.*, Principles of Marketing, *Prentice Hall, 1999*)

Figure 3.23 *Product life cycle variants*

Figure 3.23 shows three typical variants and there are many more. A cycle may be very slow to take off and then remain in the profitable maturity stage for many years. Another might soar away from its launch only to crash a few months or weeks later. This means that marketing managers must be cautious in their interpretation of sales changes and avoid over-reacting to what might be misleading data. There is also the risk of confusing product performance with changes in the external business environment. For example, a sharp rise in the rate of duty on petrol could cut UK demand for the F-type Jaguar car, which is a heavy user of fuel.

A CTIVITY

Figure 3.24 Frubes

By the 1990s Yoplait-Dairy Crest had established its Petit Filous as a leading brand of fromage frais. The challenge the company faced was to devise a new product that would increase sales by entering another segment of the market. The new product, Frubes, was launched in 1996 and put fruit-flavoured fromage frais in soft plastic tubes which could be squeezed and sucked as 'a delicious and healthy snack'. In this way fromage frais could be sold to parents for their children to eat at any time and could be designed to be added to a child's packed lunch.

Frubes were packaged in 9-tube boxes with their own distinctive logo and graphic design.

Tasks

1 How might Yoplait have generated the idea for Frubes?
2 How far could Yoplait be certain that Frubes would be a success?
3 What kind of pricing strategy might have been right for the launch of Frubes?
4 How could the model of the product life cycle help in the marketing of Frubes?

The Boston Matrix

Many firms contain more than one distinct business unit. These could be subsidiaries, product divisions or just a single product or brand. With the aim of long-term profitability, senior managers need to understand the role of each business in their portfolio as well as that of each product within those business units. In a fast-changing business environment this means considering the company's market share and the size of the overall markets.

The Boston Matrix can assist this analysis. Products are placed on a grid according to their relative market share and the growth rate of the industry concerned.

Key term

Relative market share means the firm's share of this market as compared with that of competitors.

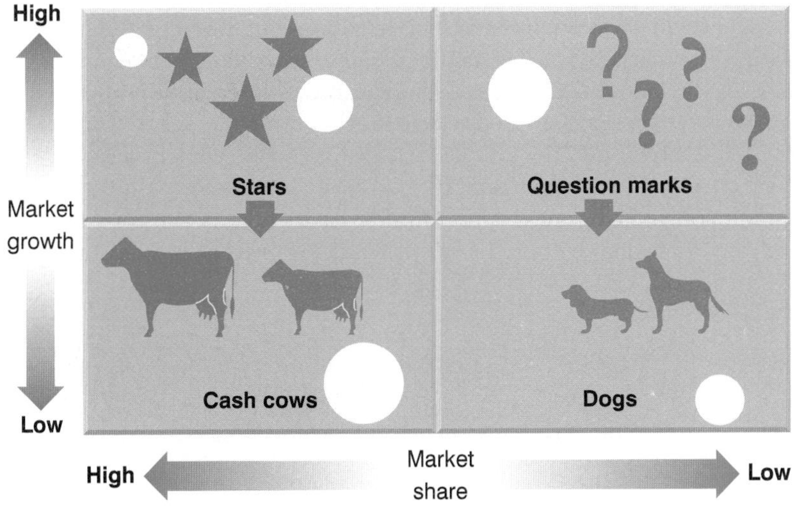

Figure 3.25 *The Boston Matrix*

The diameter of the circles representing the firm's products is proportional to sales levels. The four sections of the grid are designated:

- Stars, high market share – high industry growth rate
- Question marks, low market share – high industry growth rate
- Cash Cows, high market share – low industry growth rate
- Dogs, low market share – low industry growth rate.

Stars are products/product ranges with a high market share in a fast-growing industry. Because they are successful their source of competitive advantage is usually under strong pressure from rivals. Consequently, heavy marketing expenses are likely to be necessary for stars to maintain their position.

Question marks are products/product ranges with a small market share in a fast-growing industry. They are not very profitable but their strategic value depends on their potential in winning a larger share of the market. Managers must decide whether the product can become a star and whether the necessary marketing support is justified.

Cash cows are well-established products/product ranges with a high market share in a mature or slow growth industry. In previous life they were normally stars. They often have a strong competitive advantage and a loyal customer base. As unit costs are relatively low, profitability is high and cash cows (as their name suggests) are an important source of funding for other products.

Dogs are products/product ranges with a low share in slow growth or mature markets. If they carry low costs, they may generate enough cash to justify their retention for a time at least. Alternatively, a dog may have competitive advantage in a specialist market where higher margins ensure adequate profitability. Many previously successful cash cows and question marks have become dogs because the company continued with a product when the best strategy was to withdraw it from the market.

Look again at Figure 3.25. The firm is fortunate in having a substantial cash cow which generates enough cash to support its star and hopeful-looking question mark. The dog looks unpromising unless it is in a specialist market. This balancing of business activities between the grids in the matrix is strategically important. A different firm might have two or three products or product ranges that are stars and another two or three that are question marks. The firm as a whole might well have huge potential but there would be a seriously inadequate cash flow for the support of its business opportunities. Apart from heavy borrowing, the only solution might be the sale of some parts of the business in order to finance others.

A CTIVITY

HSBC – then Midland Bank – launched First Direct as a highly innovative telephone banking system back in 1989. There were no branches and costs were kept to a minimum. Customers were offered an automatic overdraft allowance and – the key proposition – 24-hour access to account details. During the 1990s competitors increasingly entered the market, but First Direct had the advantage of being perceived as the 'original brand'. The introduction of Internet banking in 2000 was assisted by the brand's image of innovation and reliability.

Task

1 First Direct quickly became a 'star' on the Boston Matrix. How should a star be managed?
2 How might HSBC recognise that the First Direct current account has arrived at the maturity stage of the product life cycle?
3 As competition intensifies, how might HSBC defend First Direct as a product and as a brand?

Figure 3.26 First Direct

Pricing products

The meaning of price

Price is the exchange rate placed on a product by the seller in a market. It is an exchange rate because the product is being offered to a buyer in exchange for an amount of money. In our modern economy money is a go-between. It has no value in itself, but is wanted for what it can buy: in other words for its exchange rate. So money allows one person to sell, say, a car for £1,000 and buy, say, a laptop computer for the same amount. In effect they have exchanged a car for a laptop, using money as the go-between.

In business, market price or the rate of exchange that is chosen or achieved is of utmost importance as it represents the sales revenue per unit of the product.

Sales revenue is the lifeblood of a business. Costs of the product, including its promotion and distribution, are only incurred so that they add value and generate sales revenue. To avoid losses and make a profit, sales revenue must exceed costs. This also means that the firm has added value to the inputs used in its overall production process. The exchange of costs for sales revenue is at the heart of the market mechanism and the marketing mix.

 Market, page 1

 Added value, page 43

> **Key term**
>
> The **marketing mix** is the combination of price, product, promotion and distribution (place) used by a firm to express its marketing strategy.

ASE STUDY

Which camera?

A customer has seen the advertisement for the Olympus MJU II Zoom in a Sunday supplement. He enters a branch of Dixons where the assistant admires the MJU II at £179.99 with its compact design, quality lens and automatic setting. The nearest rival would be a Canon Classic at £169.99.

The customer pauses and then decides. 'I'll buy the Olympus.'

The idea of price and value can be easily confused. Price is value achieved or expected in the marketplace. Value outside the market is a matter of personal opinion and for the same product it may vary widely. This is why – at a given market price – some customers gain greater value for money than others.

Pricing policies

Cost-plus pricing

Some firms decide their price in relation to the profit margin they want to make. The price is determined by marking up the cost of the product by the necessary percentage. This approach is called cost-plus, i.e. cost plus profit.

It is important to be clear about the arithmetic involved. A mark-up is the percentage by which the cost price of a product is increased to find the selling price. The formula for mark-up is:

$$\frac{profit}{cost\ price} \times 100$$

So for a product costing 80p, the mark up is 50 per cent of 80p = 40p and the price is 80p (cost) plus 40p (profit) = £1.20. Stanton Stationery marks up by 50 per cent. But this does not mean that its profit margin is 50 per cent.

$$\begin{aligned} profit\ margin &= \frac{profit}{selling\ price} \times 100 \\[1em] &= \frac{40p}{£1.20} \times 100 \\[1em] &= 33\ per\ cent \end{aligned}$$

CASE STUDY

Stanton Stationery Ltd

This small East Midlands company uses cost – plus pricing. When orders arrive from the wholesaler, the cost price is marked up by 50 per cent to arrive at the selling price. This gives the company a gross margin of 33 per cent. The company's owner, Dave Stanton, argues that cost-plus is simple to use, saves time and helps to make his monthly profit more predictable.

Like Stanton, many smaller firms use cost-plus as a simple way of ensuring a target rate of profit.

How is the mark-up percentage decided? As always in business, much depends on the competition. If one firm's products are readily available from local competitors, then a 'going rate' price will have developed. Suppose that this implied a mark-up of say, 25 per cent, then the corresponding profit margin would be 20 per cent (check this for yourself).

CASE STUDY

Denslow's DIY

Martin Denslow knows what local competitors charge, and knows what they pay. He is aware that the local branch of B&Q is only 20 miles away. A mark-up of 33 per cent is realistic and in line with that of competitors. Any increase in price would surely hand his customers over to rivals.

Culm Crafts

Anne Powell buys in all kinds of craft products for her gallery in Devon. She is careful to ensure that her stock is distinctive and unlike that of other craft shops. Her customers often return on successive holidays. She generally marks up by 100 per cent but admits that in the summer season she is often tempted to try for a higher rate.

ACTIVITY

Pemberton Stores

Diane and Pete Jacob run the only shop in the village of Pemberton, close to the M6 in Staffordshire. Although competition from superstores is a constant worry, the Jacobs feel that they must at least aim for a level of profit that keeps the shop running. Using a cost-plus approach to pricing, they mark up wholesale prices by 33 per cent.

1   What is the profit margin at Pemberton Stores?
2   How does a cost-plus approach to pricing help in managing a business?
3   How might variations from cost-plus pricing assist a village shop to succeed in the market?

Firms with a distinctive product may have greater choice over their mark-up rate. But even for firms of this type, there are limits. Customers still have a choice. This may not be to buy the product from a competitor, but to buy a *similar* or *related* product elsewhere. And, as always, higher margins can lead to lower sales. Remember that final profit depends not only on the margin but also on the level of sales.

Competition or market-based pricing

The principles of demand and supply are very useful when investigating how the prices of goods and services are decided. In the real business world, some firms find that they have little control over price and must charge the 'going rate'. Such firms are called price takers and are common in any market where the products of different firms are very similar, e.g. petrol, everyday retailing, basic accommodation.

In these circumstances intense competition develops. Prices are driven down as each firm tries to gain market share. Profits tend towards rock-bottom levels or just enough to stay in business. Any attempt to increase price would lead to a disastrous loss of sales. Cutting price would gain many customers but this option is limited by the need to make at least a minimum profit.

Sometimes price competition gets so fierce that a price war breaks out. Slender profits turn into losses as prices are pushed down. Some firms close and the survivors eventually raise their prices. In recent years price wars have broken out between supermarkets, airlines and oil companies.

Ⓒ**ASE STUDY**

Put a Tiger Token in your wallet

Back in 1986 Esso introduced Tiger Tokens. These were given free with petrol purchases and could be exchanged for items in a catalogue of gifts. BP operated a rival scheme for free air-miles. Meanwhile the supermarkets expanded into out-of-town sites and sold their own petrol without any gifts but at rock-bottom prices.

By 1996 the game was up. The supermarkets had grabbed one third of the petrol market. The secret of their marketing mix was price. Esso announced the end of Tiger Tokens and introduced 'Price Watch'. BP scrapped its air-miles and attached magnifying glass devices to its price indicators under the slogan 'Focus on price'. Motorists daily compared prices of the oil majors and the supermarkets. The gloves were off. Price was the name of the game.

Market-based pricing may also take advantage of situations where there is a lack of competition. For example, a village popular with tourists may have only two cafés, both of which are very crowded and able to charge high prices. In much the same way, theatres and railway buffets are able to charge 'what the market will pay' – prices well above the normal going rate.

Skimming and penetration strategies

Other options include skimming the market with a high price. This means the firm takes a high profit margin but has to accept lower sales and a correspondingly lower market share. This is often a sensible strategy for an innovative product at the introductory stage of its product life cycle. Enthusiasts can pay the price and help recoup the product's development cost. Skimming also works well in a niche market. A specialised product that is distinct from its competitors may sell to a limited range of customers who will pay a price premium.

The alternative approach is to use a lower price to achieve market penetration. This means that a lower margin is accepted in return for higher sales – and often a larger market share. This is the usual strategy for mature products in mass markets.

 **CTIVITY**

Table 3.2

Taylor's of Harrogate	Nescafé
Fine coffees and teas are imported, blended and marketed by this traditional Yorkshire-based company. Only freshly roasted beans and ground coffees are sold in distinctive packaging. Taylor's Coffee of the Month appeals to discerning coffee drinkers and is produced at £2.99 per packet (227g). By contrast Tesco's Original Blend ground coffee is priced at £1.29 per packet (227g).	Nescafé instant coffee was originally launched in 1953. It is now one of Nescafé's key brands, recognised and marketed around the world. Advertised on TV and in other media, it competes against Maxwell House and supermarket own-label brands. Nescafé appeals to a mass market and is widely distributed through supermarkets, grocers and catering outlets. Sold in a range of sizes, the 100g jar sells for £1.65. By contrast, Carte Noire instant coffee from Kenco is priced at £2.45 per 100g jar.

1 Why do you think consumers are willing to pay the price premiums for Taylor's Coffee of the Month or Kenco's Carte Noire?

2 What do you think makes Nescafé so popular? Is it the price? Or is it the product? Or the advertising? Explain your view.

 **CTIVITY**

Petrol sales

Investigate the prices being charged by your local filling stations including any supermarket petrol outlets.

1 Collect the data and make brief notes on the location of the filling stations and any other facilities that they offer, e.g. a shop or repair workshop.

2 Find as many factors as possible to explain (a) the similarity of prices and (b) any differences in price. Brainstorm ideas using your knowledge of pricing. Try to interview at least one filling station manager.

3 Using any evidence from your investigation, attempt to answer the following questions:

   i) How would you describe the pricing methods for petrol?

   ii) How competitive is the petrol market?

   iii) How do firms marketing petrol try to gain a competitive advantage?

| Product analysis

What is a product?

The basic aim of a seller is to alert buyers to their product and to persuade them that a purchase represents the best value. When considering whether to buy a product, customers weigh up the price against the expected benefits. Is the product worth the price?

C ASE STUDY

Figure 3.27 *Tenerife – or not?*

Kimberley Davis looked hard at the Lunn Poly brochure. £299 was a lot to part with. She thought about clothes and driving lessons. Her eyes moved back to the brochure. Modern hotel with luxury swimming pool. Direct flight from Manchester. No hidden extras. Sun-soaked days and fun-filled nights, it promised. But it still seemed a lot of money.

It is worth thinking for a moment, what is a product? We tend to assume that the answer is obvious: the goods or services on offer. But people actually buy products for the benefits they yield – now or in the future. A washing machine is not bought for itself but for the benefit of having clothes conveniently washed. A pair of shoes are bought for their comfort and style. Even a night at a hotel is a 'bundle' of benefits – a bedroom, breakfast, use of the lounges and bars, perhaps even a sense of status and prestige. For marketing managers this insight is important. Instead of simply selling a product, as though its specification and character were fixed, managers can break down its benefits and analyse them one by one.

One result of thorough product analysis is a much improved understanding of what a product *really* is to its buyers. Quite often a firm may not fully understand its own product. Managers may be expert on technical matters and know exactly how their product compares with the competition. But they may not know fully the product's emotional and psychological appeal. Perhaps surprisingly this is often a key source of added value and competitive advantage.

CASE STUDY

The twist-wrapped flake bar was introduced in 1925 and has sold well ever since. But modern automated packaging systems mean that twist wrapping is costly and inconvenient. A simple crimped closure of the film material would be more efficient.

Yet market research shows that consumers have many ways of eating a Flake, including breaking and crumbling the bar for increased eating pleasure. The twist wrapping is actually an important element in the product's long-lasting appeal.

Figure 3.28 Cadbury's Flake

How can product value be increased?

By unbundling the sources of value in a product, a firm can analyse the sources of the product's profitability and evaluate its place in the market. Remember that a product's success depends on the difference between its costs and its market value. Each product feature can be assessed. What is its contribution to the market value? What does it cost to include or maintain? The answers to these questions may then trigger further research and investigation. Could the appeal of a particular feature be increased at relatively little cost? Or could the cost of a feature be reduced with relatively little loss of appeal?

CASE STUDY

Time Off

Time Off is a small UK travel company specialising in short continental and US city centre breaks. The holidays, though not necessarily luxurious, emphasise quality and personal service. For example, clients are sent exact details of their individual travel schedule with maps and useful guides. Typically a hotel may leave a small gift in the guest's bedroom. These 'touches' of quality are not actually very costly but they are often highly valued by the customer.

Some firms bring together questions of this type within a process of product value analysis. Market research is fed into the evaluation of product features which are assessed for cost and value.

ⒸASE STUDY

Thinner or thicker?

Thinner	Thicker
A biscuit manufacturer decides to reduce the thickness of milk chocolate coatings in its Family Assortment. The cost saving is significant and it is expected that a reduction in price will outweigh any customer disappointment.	A producer of luxury chocolates decides to increase the thickness of cardboard used in their boxes. It is expected that the gain in customer satisfaction will outweigh any small increase in costs and price.

It is wrong to assume that value analysis leads to cost-cutting and reduced quality. Value analysis can point in the opposite direction. In fact the whole exercise needs creative flair and a real sense of empathy with the customers' experiences and feelings.

There should also be a note of caution about value analysis. For some products the 'whole' is greater than the sum of the 'parts'. Products and brands have a kind of integrity that may be damaged through changes in their appearance or identity.

Classic products

This is particularly relevant for 'classic' products and brands where lack of change is part of the mystique and appeal. In a sense, the product is already as good as it can ever be. Think of a Swiss Army penknife. This is a superbly designed top-quality product manufactured to the highest specifications. The range of penknives is adjusted, but the essential product remains the same. Such products and brands are immensely valuable.

ⒸASE STUDY

The product: Lyle's Golden Syrup

Lyle's Golden Syrup is still sold in a real tin with graphics that date back to the 1920s. This is a classic product which no one wants to change. Nothing else is as good.

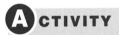 ASE STUDY

The brand: Coca-Cola

Coca-Cola is the king of soft drinks, the ultimate all-American brand. Back in 1985 the company replaced its famous product with 'New Coke'. The result was a marketing disaster. 'Classic Coke' was hastily restored. (Pepsi are still laughing.)

Try imagining Golden Syrup in a cheap plastic tub with bright blue graphics. Supposing Coca-Cola abandoned its red livery and produced green tins one month and purple tins another – what would happen then?

Figure 3.29 *A classic product may give birth to new stars*

A classic product may become a very long-life cash cow and even give birth to new stars – for example, Golden Syrup cake bars.

A CTIVITY

The Golden Fleece

Dating back to Elizabethan times, the Golden Fleece is a 35-bedroom hotel set in the heart of an old Suffolk town. It was recently purchased by Sundial Ltd, a growing chain of specialist hotels. The firm's marketing is focused on upmarket short-break holidays and small-scale business conferences. Maureen Ward, Sundial's marketing director, feels that The Golden Fleece has potential for hosting special events such as wedding receptions and retirement dinners. Staff at the hotel are generally loyal and long-serving.

After less than a month of new ownership, The Golden Fleece is visited by John Stride, Sundial's company accountant. He has examined the hotel's accounts and is dissatisfied with its financial performance. Though room occupancy rates are good he believes costs are too high. The staff are well motivated and conscientious but, according to John, spend a lot of time polishing old tables and chatting with elderly guests. John has also scrutinised the hotel's inventory. He calculates that up to £50,000 could be released for improvements to the car park if half the antiques are sold.

 Cash cows, page 35

Tasks

1 When guests stay at The Golden Fleece for a short break, what kind of 'product' are they buying?
2 What are the likely sources of competitive advantage for (a) Sundial Ltd and (b) The Golden Fleece?
3 How might The Golden Fleece modify its product offering to attract small-scale business conferences?
4 How might Maureen Ward respond to John Stride's observations?

Promoting the product

What is product promotion?

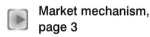

Market mechanism, page 3

Every effort to make a product or brand seem more attractive or valuable is a form of product promotion. Think about the market mechanism and the relationship between demand and supply. The strength of consumer demand depends on the positive gap between what a product appears to be worth and the price actually charged. Product promotion is all about prising open the 'jaws' of value for money.

Promotion and value for money

There are many different ways of persuading consumers that they are achieving value for money. Branding, packaging and presentation change perceptions of the product. Advertising communicates with the target market and aims not only to increase sales but also to increase the valuation of the product by consumers. Personal selling presents the product to individuals with the aim of promoting sales. Finally customer service supports the customer's needs at and after the time of purchase.

Branding

A brand is a recognisable identity for a product or range of products. Branding dates back to the Middle Ages but developed in its modern form during the nineteenth century when factory production and better transport enabled producers to market their products on a national basis. Brands usually develop from a particularly successful firm or product: Coca-Cola, Kodak or Volkswagen, for example. The firm or product becomes associated by consumers with desirable factors such as quality, durability or style. These qualities become attached to the name, logo or characteristic design and a brand develops.

Table 3.3 *Britain's top ten grocery brands 1999*

Rank	Brand	Sales value £m
1	Coca-Cola	396
2	Nescafé	356
3	Walkers Crisps	344
4	Persil	238
5	Andrex	220
6	Pampers	201
7	Müller Pot Desserts	198
8	Ariel	182
9	Robinsons	154
10	Sunny Delight	150

Source: Marketing Pocket Book 2001 (NTC Publications)

Brands are usually represented by a name or logo. They are often reinforced by a livery (brand colours) and a distinctive design style. For example, Kodak is recognised by its yellow-gold livery while Apple computers are known for their stylish and user-friendly design.

 Marketing mix, page 37

As part of the marketing mix, brands are increasingly important because they can command:

- added value
- increased market share
- entry to distribution channels.

Because consumers identify brands as having desirable qualities, any product carrying the brand gains extra value in the market. Since the brand is exclusive to the firm, it becomes an important source of competitive advantage. Successful brands allow a price premium which adds greatly to business profitability.

Strong brands are effective in gaining market share as they offer consumers consistent and recognisable value for money. Consumers feel safe in purchasing a well known brand. This in turn means that wholesalers and retailers want to stock the product.

Brands can also have a strategic value in allowing firms to enter new markets and to diversify their product range. This is because the essence of a good brand is transferable. Qualities such as reliability or good value can be applied to any product. It was this factor that enabled Marks & Spencer to diversify from clothing and food into household goods and personal finance.

ASE STUDY

Virgin territory?

Thirty years ago records were mostly sold from small, family-owned stores. When Richard Branson launched Virgin Records as a discount mail-order operation in 1970, his full-page advertisement in *Melody Maker* urged readers to 'bung a tick' against the records of their choice. Unknown to him, a brand was in the making.

Young, cheap, fast-moving, different, daring: these were and are the essential qualities of the Virgin brand. They have allowed Richard Branson to use his initial success in the record industry as a bridgehead for entering markets in entertainment, video, air travel, soft drinks, pensions and railways. Many new markets are Virgin territory!

The power of a brand can be eroded or damaged through errors by the firm. Brands need products that justify their reputation and support from advertising and other elements in the marketing mix. The 'integrity' of a brand needs defending against any threats. For example, McDonalds and all fast-food restaurants must be extremely careful that their products are never publicly linked with cases of food poisoning.

CASE STUDY

Persil Power

Persil is an established, well-trusted brand. The launch of Persil Automatic back in the 1960s was a massive marketing success. In 1993 Lever Bros (the brand owner) launched new formula Persil Power. But soon the rival company, Procter & Gamble, were publicly claiming that Persil Power's active ingredient actually damaged the fabric of clothing.

Independent surveys supported Procter & Gamble. Supermarkets began to remove Persil Power from their shelves. A disaster was unfolding. Six months after the launch, Persil Power was withdrawn at a loss to Lever Bros of £60 million.

Strong brands have become extremely valuable. Cadbury-Schweppes currently values its brands at over £1,600 million (more than the value of all land, buildings and machinery owned by the company) while an increasing number of takeover bids are motivated by the attractiveness of other firms' brands.

Packaging

There are two basic purposes of packaging:

- functional
- persuasive.

Essential protection for many products is provided by packaging. It allows intended quantities of the product to reach the consumer in perfect condition. The risks of theft, tampering and waste are all reduced. The packaging may also have further value in dispensing and storing the product while carrying important instructions for the consumer's guidance.

Packaging is a very significant source of added value. On average, packaging represents around 10 per cent of a product's price but this value can be much higher for luxury goods – as high as 40 per cent for cosmetics. These costs are far higher than would be necessary to meet the protective functions of packaging. What additional benefits is the firm producing and selling?

ACTIVITY

Each of the packaging solutions shown in Figure 3.30 protects and stores the product. How do you think each package adds further value to the product inside?

Figure 3.30 *Examples of packaging*

Modern packaging techniques allow projection of the brand and careful building of the product's intended image. It promotes the product at the point of sale while playing an important role in differentiating the product from its competitors. There is also the potential to use package size and style to penetrate different market segments. For example, orange juice is cheapest in one litre boxes but the small 25cl cartons have proved very popular to go with snacks and packed lunches.

Want to know more?

Pure gold?

'All that glisters is not gold' is a famous Shakespearean quotation but the associative power of gold to suggest luxury and wealth shows no sign of diminishing. As a brand, Benson and Hedges cigarettes are virtually built on the image of 'Gold'. Terry's All Gold chocolates remain a top brand after more than sixty years. Most banks offer 'gold' cards while building societies come up with 'gold accounts'.

Other colours have psychological significance too. Black is linked with power, white with purity, purple with indulgence, green with nature and red with excitement. Some brands adopt colours with exactly these associations in mind.

In many cases it would be hard to think of the product without its elaborate packaging. Exclusive perfume or Scotch whisky are obvious examples. But what do customers want when they buy a can of Coke?

The can (and its social messages) or the Coke (just a fizzy drink)? The power of packaging to interest, satisfy or delight the customer is very real.

Advertising

When any product is taken to the marketplace, it must be announced to likely customers. The cries of stallholders at a traditional open-air market are an unsophisticated form of advertising. In modern markets where consumers rarely meet producers and every product must compete for attention against so many others, the role of advertising has never been greater.

The effect of advertising is to increase sales or allow for a higher price or a combination of both. In some cases advertising is necessary just to stand still. Competition may be so intense that failure to advertise will lead to erosion of sales and brand loyalty. This is the argument used by many firms producing fast-moving consumer goods (often abbreviated to 'fmcg') to justify high advertising expenditure.

How much does advertising influence buying behaviour? There is no single answer, since much depends on the product and the quality of the advertising. But there is no doubt that advertising can change consumer perceptions and behaviour. Research from the USA has shown that it is easier to change simple buying behaviour than it is to shift underlying attitudes towards a product. In other words, advertising may persuade consumers to try a product or – for a time – to use it more often. But their deeper beliefs and values are much less readily affected by the efforts of advertisers. For example, advertising might well affect a consumer's choice of Galaxy or Cadbury's Dairy Milk, but would be unlikely to change their view that chocolate should be a rare luxury.

As a part of the marketing mix, firms must assign to advertising clear objectives and an appropriate budget. A small package holiday firm might want advertising to inform customers within a market segment that they have an alternative choice. An established major operator might be more anxious to persuade the market that its hotels offer superior facilities at an unbeatably low price.

Almost all larger firms employ a specialist advertising agency. The agency's task is to interpret the firm's strategy, understand the essence of the product and devise an advertising campaign that is most likely to fulfil the client's objectives.

This may be rational in communicating the product's *objective* qualities such as function, power, size or colours. In most cases the message is also emotional and conveys *subjective* arguments and associations. These may encourage consumers to feel good by buying the product or to *avoid* feeling bad. Moral appeals are widely used by charities in advertising their cause.

To be effective, an advertiser's message should attract attention, stimulate interest, create desire and result in action (i.e. purchase of the product). This framework for designing advertisements is known as A-I-D-A:

Marketing mix, page 37

- Attention
- Interest
- Desire
- Action.

The choice of advertising medium is very important to the success of any campaign. The main choices are:

Table 3.4 Advertising media

Type	Examples	Typical subject
Broadcast	TV (commercial)	Consumer goods and services (mainstream)
	TV (satellite & cable)	Consumer goods and services (segmented)
	Cinema	National brands and local retailing
	Internet websites	Information
	Radio	Local retailers and agents
Print	Newspapers	Retailing and brand building
	Magazines	Promotional offers
	Leaflets	
Display	Billboards	Brand promotion
	Posters	Brand promotion
	Signs	Outlet awareness

Table 3.5 UK advertising expenditure (1999)

	%
Newspapers and magazines (including classified)	58.3
Television	32.2
Billboards and transport	4.8
Radio	3.8
Cinema	0.9
	100.0

Source: Marketing Pocket Book, 2001 (NTC Publications)

The cost of these media varies widely. Commercial television is the most expensive and is only likely to be practical for large firms with major brands. All advertising is subject to 'waste' where it fails to address the target segments. Equally media vary greatly in their 'reach': the number of consumers in their relevant audience. The advertising agency has the specialist knowledge to guide a firm in the best use of its budget.

Sales promotion

Sales promotion is a collective term for all the promotional activities carried out by firms apart from advertising and personal selling. It works at consumer, trade and business levels and needs careful co-ordination with the distribution channels. Typical methods include:

Distribution channels, page 55

- tactical price reductions where products are flashed with a 'special price' or a reduction; this may take the form of additional quantity for the same price: '20 per cent extra', 'two for the price of one' or 'buy one, get one free'
- coupons offering 'money off' products, which is a more targeted approach to price reductions and the consumer redeems them at the time of purchase
- free samples distributed in-store or by post; this method may persuade consumers to try a product at the introduction stage in its life cycle; alternatively firms may offer 'free gifts' with their product. Advertising specialities may also be available such as mugs or clothing carrying the brand name and company logo
- loyalty cards which give regular consumers extra benefits as rewards for purchasing such as 'free' products or air miles
- competitions requiring postal entries from consumers with 'proof of purchase' and which regularly promise cash awards or exotic prizes.

Merchandising and point-of-sales displays

The point-of-sale is the 'front line' in any marketing strategy. This is the final point of decision. The consumer is confronted with the choice of buying the firm's product, a competitor's product or neither. The promotional mix follows the consumer right up to this point.

> **Key term**
>
> **Promotional mix** means a firm's chosen combination of advertising, branding, packaging and other techniques of sales promotion designed to encourage purchase of the product.

ACTIVITY

In the following two examples suggest a sales promotion strategy for each product to cover the first six months after launch.

Jupiter by Mars

Mars is thinking of launching a new chocolate fudge and caramel bar called Jupiter. It aims to sell alongside Mars bars and Milky Way, appealing mainly to under 25s.

Sony Club 2000

Sony decides to launch a new micro-size hi-fi called Club 2000. It will be priced around £200, and have a high power output and improved 'mega-bass' feature. The target market is students aged 14–24.

Merchandising involves ensuring that products are prominently and attractively displayed in order to maximise sales.

It has grown in importance as shops have abandoned traditional 'counters' in favour of allowing customers to roam around the store and pay for selections at island-style tills or checkouts. Representatives of the producer often work with the retail staff in making merchandising decisions. Many producers supply point-of-sale display units, posters and other publicity to help secure sales. In larger stores the retailer usually maintains a 'house style' that is closely associated with a brand; for example, think of the layout and styling at Dixons or WH Smith. Often, displays by specific manufacturers will be expected to match the increasingly sophisticated standards of large retailers.

> **Key term**
>
> **Mechandising** is the presentation of goods in retail outlets with a view to maximising their sales.

ASE STUDY

Frozen out of the village

One Devon seaside village found that it had three outlets for ice cream, all offering Wall's. Yet the village was also home to a local ice-cream producer who had won national awards for quality and flavour. This ice cream was not available in the village.

One reason was that retailers were offered refrigerated display cabinets by Wall's on the condition that these were not used to store the products of other firms. Shopkeepers also argued that Wall's was a national brand and better known to customers through its television advertising. A ruling from the Department of Trade and Industry in 2000 meant that in future 50 per cent of the space in a Wall's freezer must be available for the products of other ice-cream manufacturers.

Customer service

Customer service tends to be most noticeable when absent or lacking. The best customer service fits seamlessly with the product, completing the production chain. It critically adds value to a product and is important in securing a sale. At one extreme, most DIY warehouses employ relatively few staff since most customers prefer to make their own choices and ask for information as required. By contrast, most quality hotels employ plenty of staff since personal service is a vital part of their 'product'. Customer service at a garage may involve listening attentively to the customer's description of the car's faults and then providing a free courtesy car service to minimise inconvenience.

A CTIVITY

Assisting sales?

Customer: 'Do you have Product X in stock?'
Sales Assistant A: 'No.'
Sales Assistant B: 'No, I'm sorry, we don't.'
Sales Assisant C: 'No, I'm sorry, we don't. But I'll check for you. And if not, I can order it now and telephone you as soon as it arrives.'

Task

How can a sales assistant add value?

In outlets that are part of a national or international chain, customer service directly represents the brand. Outstanding service strengthens competitive advantage while poor service does immense damage. This is why the major supermarket chains not only offer 'no quibble' refunds on returned goods but may also offer twice their value. By being among the first of clothing retailers to offer friendly unconditional refunds on returned goods, Marks & Spencer built an enviable reputation for customer service and fair trading.

Training and motivating sales staff has increased in importance as customers' expectations have risen and the competitive edge represented by customer service has sharpened.

C ASE STUDY

Great Western delight

First Great Western is one of the train operating companies set up under the terms of rail privatisation. The case was recently reported of a passenger travelling to Exeter who left his coat on a train while changing at Reading. The Great Western Help Desk immediately contacted the train's next stop at Swindon and arranged for staff to remove the coat which was then dispatched on another service to Exeter where it would await collection. The passenger was delighted by this standard of service.

Distributing the product

What is distribution?

No matter how well designed, well promoted or attractively priced, a product has no chance of success unless it reaches the market. Sellers need to engage effectively with their potential buyers – often through a wide range of channels.

CASE STUDY

Rabid Badger

This small record label is fiercely independent yet it has a distribution deal with EMI. Back in the 1990s Creation Records, famous for having had the foresight to sign Oasis, also depended on distribution deals with major labels. The reason is simple. Small independent record labels exploit their skills to discover new artists and to make records. These creative processes can be highly successful on a small scale. But the vital task of distribution to music stores in this country and abroad needs a large-scale operation with major financial resources. Distribution deals with much larger firms is what has enabled the likes of Rabid Badger and Creation to flourish.

The distribution channel is the way a product passes through various organisations between production and consumption. Why do most firms use the services of other companies to get their products to the market? The answer lies partly in the fact that firms generally produce a fairly narrow range of goods or services in large quantities. By contrast, most consumers want to select from a wide range of goods and services. This mismatch of wishes is resolved by firms in the distribution business.

There is also a powerful business reason. Increasingly, successful firms keep their resources focused on those activities in which they have a competitive advantage. Distribution, including retailing, has itself become a highly specialised industry that is driven by the market to be efficient and innovative. Most firms recognise that they could not compete with the well established distributors and that they can gain by handing over this part of the marketing mix.

In Figure 3.31 it can be seen that without a distributor 12 different contracts and joining pathways are necessary. Once a distributor is involved, the number of network connections falls to seven.

Many distribution channels are possible. The most common in consumer marketing are shown in Figure 3.32.

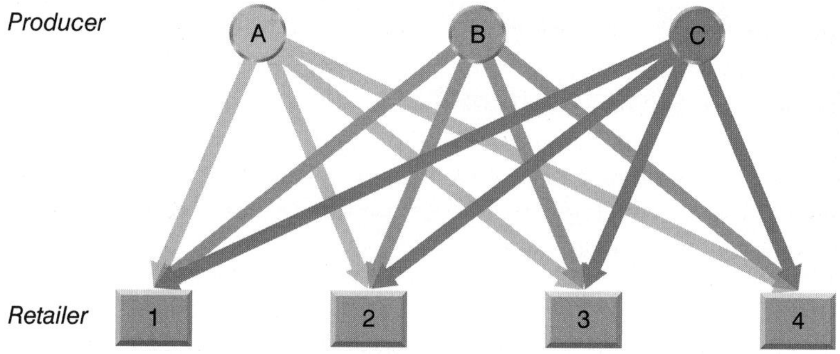

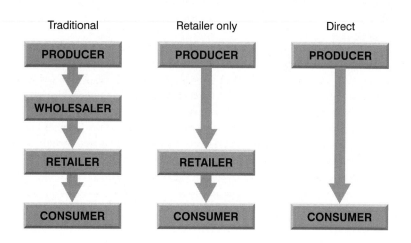

Figure 3.31 *Increased efficiency using a distributor*

Figure 3.32 *Typical distribution channels*

As always, the best choice for a producer depends on the balance between cost and benefit. The 'middleman' in distribution carries some important tasks:

- packaging
- transport of goods
- promotion of merchandising
- financing the distribution for the market
- stockholding at each stage
- collecting market intelligence.

Taken together, these activities add value to the product (consider the value of unwrapped butter, only available from a warehouse on the M1!) which is reflected in the price mark-ups made by the wholesaler and retailer.

Eliminating the wholesaler and selling direct to the retailer can be a good strategy when a higher degree of control over the final sale is required and the number of retailers is limited. Similarly, cutting out all the middlemen and selling a product direct to the consumer (e.g. craft products and factory outlets) can make sense when direct contact with the customer is important. But it is worth remembering that the distribution functions have still to be performed in one form or another.

The marketing manager needs to decide on the market coverage of distribution. Intensive distribution ensures that the product reaches every possible sales outlet. This is the approach of firms producing fast-moving consumer goods. Cadburys, Coca-Cola, Hovis and McVities are brands that need extensive distribution. Other products are better suited to selective distribution, meaning that only certain outlets are chosen to carry the product. This is often the policy of publishers and makers of electrical goods. Costs are reduced and a closer relationship with dealers and retailers allows more control over the final selling process. For some luxury goods, producers prefer exclusive distribution where only specially appointed dealers can sell their product. Upmarket cars, jewellery and clothing are often distributed in this way. The image-value of the brand is strengthened and dealers' merchandising environment can be checked for suitability.

Traditional distribution systems are based on physical movement of goods from producer to consumer. Towards the turn of this century the emphasis shifted towards market logistics. This approach starts with the customer and works back – not only to the producer but also further back up the value chain to the firm's suppliers.

A market logistics manager has responsibility for movements along the whole production chain as it affects the firm. The logistics approach is strongly market oriented and aims to deliver customer satisfaction through efficiency in the whole supply chain.

> **Key term**
>
> **Market logistics** are a sequence of activities in the process of production, each of which adds value to the goods and services concerned.

CASE STUDY

Sorry, it's out of stock

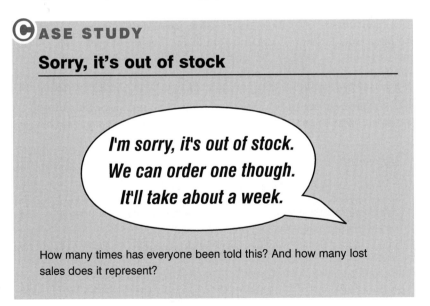

I'm sorry, it's out of stock. We can order one though. It'll take about a week.

How many times has everyone been told this? And how many lost sales does it represent?

By using computer technology many firms aim to eliminate time-lags in the availability of their products. Customer demand puts pressure on businesses and ensures that resources are allocated throughout the supply chain. When businesses respond to demand in this way, resources are pulled through the system to meet production and delivery schedules.

This process of allocating resources extends from suppliers, through the manufacturing process and onwards, along distribution channels.

Viking Direct

This catalogue-based company sells office stationery 'direct' through telephone orders. Customer satisfaction is taken very seriously. Although the marketing proposition is based strongly on low price, other elements in the marketing mix are not forgotten. The moment a customer's order is accepted, the Viking distribution process swings into action and delivery is guaranteed within 24 hours. A sophisticated computer system using postcodes directs a fleet of Viking vans from a central warehouse. A flexible arrangement with Parcels Express allows Viking to keep that delivery promise when orders reach unexpected peaks. In this way, Ian Helford, the chairman, argues that customers enjoy warehouse prices and the convenience of almost immediate delivery.

Wholesalers

Wholesalers buy from producers in bulk and sell to retailers in smaller quantities. They add to costs but can also add to value. A wholesaler's most basic job is the breaking of bulk deliveries from manufacturers into the much smaller orders needed by retailers. This is not only convenient but also saves the expense for retailers of holding excessive stocks. Many wholesalers draw together a wide range of goods according to the pattern of demand from their retail customers. They may also provide retailers with valuable advice on handling and selling the products, including help with store layout, displays and customer service.

Happy Shopper

Ask most people if they've heard of 'Booker' and most likely they'll say 'No.' But they have heard of Happy Shopper. This is the brand name under which the wholesaler, Booker, markets a range of groceries and household goods to the retail trade. Many of the customers at Booker's cash-and-carry stores are sole traders who run small convenience stores or village shops. For them, the Happy Shopper name is valuable. Stocking a brand that customers recognise and associate with everyday good value helps them to compete with the supermarkets. The cash-and-carry also provides the right mix of products available immediately in the small quantities that sole traders usually need.

Figure 3.33

Retailing

Retailing is the sale of goods and services by a business to the final consumer. Traditionally, 'shopping' meant buying a variety of products from a large number of stores – mostly independently owned – in a town or city centre. Increasingly today, 'shopping' can mean using the car to visit an out-of-town superstore or shopping mall where the business owners are national or international companies. Visits to the High Street are becoming more like a leisure activity with the retail emphasis on speciality products. Meanwhile Internet shopping is on the increase.

These trends reflect major changes in consumers' lifestyles and tastes. Retailers track these changes and respond so as to ensure they maintain or improve their competitive position. Retailing provides consumers with choice, display, convenience and personal service. But each of these benefits has a cost. Each retailer must decide on the right mix of benefits and the right corresponding price.

Retailers offering extensive customer service tend to have costly facilities and staffing. These tend to be department stores or specialist shops (such as Benetton or Next) which aim to offer a stylish and expensively designed environment with personal service from well trained staff. At the other end of the spectrum, self-service stores stress low prices and easy parking at their cheaper, out-of-town locations. Here the environment is functional and the staff may be helpful but are unlikely to have any detailed knowledge of the products on sale. No one type of retailing is better than another. Each mix of costs and customer benefits is best suited to a different market.

CASE STUDY

IKEA

IKEA is a Swedish retailer of furniture and household goods. Founded in 1949, it now has over 100 superstores in 25 countries and annual sales worth £4 billion to 100 million customers. The formula is simple. A standard range of simple but classic Swedish designs sells equally well all over the world. Low-cost materials are used and huge orders are placed with suppliers, enabling the firm to keep its prices about 30 per cent lower than those of comparable competitors.

Costs are further cut through the marketing mix. The stores are vast but situated on cheap sites with ample parking. Most of the goods are flat-packed and are collected from the warehouse by customers who take them home for self-assembly. Staff are well trained but few in number, only offering to help when asked.

Tesco v Levi's

In 1997 Tesco began purchasing Levi's jeans in the USA and selling them at a discount through its UK supermarkets. Far from welcoming increased sales, Levi's refused to supply Tesco and responded angrily to suggestions that its products were overpriced in Levi's official franchised stores. Higher prices were justified, argued Levi's, as the official stores offered a quality sales environment and customer guidance.

1 When a customer buys a pair of Levi's jeans, is he or she buying anything apart from an item of clothing? If so, what?

2 Why might Levi's try to control the quality of the sales environment?

3 What factors may have made Levi's resistant to Tesco selling their jeans at a discount?

Other trends in distribution

The problem with the traditional distribution channels based on the wholesale and retail trades is the involvement of different firms, each aiming to make a profit. The producer loses control over the selling process and opportunities for cost-cutting are often lost. One answer has been the growth of vertical marketing systems where the producer keeps much stronger control over the channel as a whole. The simplest method is outright ownership of the distribution channel. For example, oil companies often own petrol stations just as breweries own pubs. Some very large firms with powerful market share can specify tight terms for the sale of their products without needing to own the outlets; for example, most stationers want to sell Parker pens; most electrical stores want to stock Sony products.

Franchising is an alternative approach. This entails a contract between the owner of the brand and retail format – called the franchisor – and the operator of the outlet – called the franchisee. Firms such as Pizza Express, Burger King and Body Shop all keep strict control over the standards maintained by their franchisees.

The fastest growing trend of all is the growth of e-commerce. Use of the Internet is creating an alternative distribution system where buyers have a far wider choice of supplier, often with less regard for geographical location. Increasing volumes of e-commerce sales are being shipped through company or outsourced distributors or on a customised basis for individual transactions.

Direct marketing

Producers selling their products direct to the final consumer are involved in direct marketing. This is a growing sector that has been driven forward by the new information technologies. Computer databases enable firms to identify and communicate with increasingly small and detailed market segments. In Britain the ACORN, A Classification Of Residential Neighbourhoods, enables firms to target residential neighbourhoods all over the country with certain key characteristics. For instance, an upmarket gardening catalogue might be sent only to owners of semi-detached and detached houses in prosperous areas.

The main communication method is the direct mailing of catalogues, letters, free samples and entries to promotional competitions. Mailings are relatively cheap and are easily customised to meet the likely needs of particular consumers. Response rates can be monitored continuously with additional mailings to active customers. Magazines and TV can also offer direct marketing services by post or phone.

Selling products by phoning potential customers is called telemarketing and has proved successful in some industries – replacement windows, for example. Home shopping on TV is offered by firms such as QVC but has been slow to make a major impact in Europe. Meanwhile, computer-based electronic shopping is becoming far more important. The Internet offers a vast range of goods and services with interactive virtual shopping where customers can enter 'shops' and examine merchandise on their own private computer screen.

Marketing to existing customers

Many firms emphasise retaining and building a long-term relationship with their new and existing customers. This strategy is called relationship marketing.

Sales to retained customers are significantly more profitable than sales to a continually changing customer base. This is because the marketing cost of winning new customers is very high while sales to existing customers are more likely to be based on reputation and command a higher profit margin.

Relationship marketing usually involves a firm in offering excellent customer service and protecting every aspect of its reputation. Customer details are collected on a database where rapid and continuous computer analysis allows detailed segmentation of markets. This means that direct marketing and other promotions can be designed in a range of styles and guided towards a real relationship with individual customers. The 'loyalty cards' offered by supermarkets and chain stores form a basis for relationship marketing.

> **Key term**
>
> **Relationship marketing** means establishing ongoing relationships between a firm and its customers within which customised marketing is possible.

A CTIVITY

In 2000 Safeway stopped using its loyalty cards. Some other supermarkets followed. Why do you think these businesses took this decision?

| Marketing constraints

Is marketing moral?

Market orientation means focusing on the wants of the consumer. Marketing is about understanding and fulfilling consumer wants at prices that yield good value for the buyer and a fair profit for the seller. This sounds fine but actually the process of marketing throws up some difficult questions about right and wrong.

- Should firms be persuading people to buy products that may harm them or other people?
- How far is it acceptable to use marketing techniques in manipulating people's feelings?

Problems of this type are tackled in the study of business ethics. Take the product first. Can a firm sell anything? Clearly the answer to this question is 'no'. The law prohibits or restricts the sale of some products – for example, dangerous drugs or firearms. But things become more questionable when the product is lawful but likely to be harmful when used. Cigarettes are a classic example. They are likely to harm the buyer. They may possibly harm anyone who is a passive smoker. They are known to cost society millions of pounds in health care. Many other products raise similar questions.

> **Key term**
>
> **Business ethics** means standards of honesty and morality in conducting business affairs.

CTIVITY

Good products?

A, a manufacturer, aims to excite children with an especially realistic toy machine gun.

B, a frozen foods company, develops a new product for its 'budget' range containing high levels of unhealthy animal fats.

C, a leading car-maker, runs a poster campaign to stress the breathtaking acceleration and top speed of a new model.

D, a firm making upmarket furnishings, buys a consignment of tropical hardwood from Brazil.

E, a tobacco company, targets very poor countries in Africa with a view to increasing sales of cigarettes.

Task

What ethical problems can you recognise in each of these examples?

A basic purpose of marketing is to change people's behaviour. Attracting consumers to brands, increasing their consumption of a product, building their loyalty, identifying their dreams and fantasies: all these are attempted through different elements of the marketing mix. But is it fair for firms to use modern psychology in targeting people's weaknesses? Is it right to use sophisticated advertising to arouse needs that people never knew they had? Should salesmen be forced to use 'hard-sell' techniques that lead to people making purchases out of embarrassment or just tiredness in trying to resist?

Questions of business ethics have become more prominent in recent years, partly because firms want to avoid costly legal action. For example, companies that supplied products containing the dangerous mineral asbestos faced heavy claims for damages from former employees. In addition, most companies are very concerned about their reputation and want their brand to be associated with quality and customer satisfaction. Bad publicity may affect long-term sales.

What is the case against marketing?

Marketing is criticised from many angles. Often there is no single 'right' answer and much depends on personal points of view. Until the 1960s it was often assumed that anything lawful was acceptable. Since that time consumers have become much more sophisticated and discerning. Major firms are now very anxious to assure customers of their honest intentions.

The charges levelled by critics can be grouped under a number of headings.

Marketing and especially advertising are a waste of money

Firms are said to waste money on advertising, branding and packaging when the product itself – often called the finished product – could be sold at a much lower price. For example, in the market for cleaning products and toiletries, it is common for 40 per cent of the price to represent marketing costs.

In their defence, firms argue that marketing expenses bring intangible but real benefits to consumers. People like advertised brands and are willing to pay extra. Advertising also sharpens competition and by increasing sales allows firms to produce on a larger scale at lower cost.

Efforts are made to deceive the customer

Some firms offer a 'special purchase' or 'rock-bottom factory prices' while actually charging at least the going rate. Packaging may be cleverly designed to give an inflated impression of quality. Claims in advertising and labelling may be legal but still misleading.

Youth in a pot

According to a survey by the consumer magazine *Which?*, anti-ageing face creams are not better than ordinary moisturisers. The creams – with extra ingredients – could cost up to 75 times as much as a moisturiser yet were shown in tests on volunteer women to be almost completely ineffective.

Marketing can put unfair pressure on consumers

Door-to-door sales staff can make people feel obliged to buy. Staff from replacement window companies, for example, can be very persistent, both in telephone selling and on the doorstep. Advertisements that target children often aim to achieve sales by putting pressure on parents.

Marketing promotes harmful products

Some products, such as cigarettes, are obviously a danger to health. Many other products can be unsafe depending on how they are used.

Less obviously the major banks send out millions of mailshots urging people to take out loans for the purchase of 'dream' products. In rare cases, firms market products that are faulty or simply dangerous. This is illegal and any company with a good reputation will take immediate steps to recall the product and correct the design. Problems can arise where laws vary between countries.

Marketing may prevent competition

Small firms wanting to break into a new market often face formidable barriers to entry. Large companies may have exclusive deals with suppliers or distributors which keep out possible competitors. High advertising costs – especially through television – may mean that smaller firms cannot gain a foothold in the market. Pricing may also be used to eliminate competitors. A large firm may deliberately cut prices to such a low level that its challenger – who has fewer resources – is driven out of the market. Price then returns to the old level. Sometimes larger firms simply buy their smaller rivals. This ends unwelcome competition and helps to keep up prices. It also reduces choice for the customer.

In theory the law provides some protection against most of these strategies for reducing competition. In practice many cases are hard to prove and others escape undetected.

Marketing damages the environment

Many products have damaging effects on the environment. A car offers convenient travel and for some people is important as a status symbol. But does the price reflect the real cost to the environment?

CASE STUDY

Manufacturing a car uses scarce raw materials and large amounts of energy. Its marketing involves long-distance transportation as well as glossy brochures and pages of advertising. In use the car burns fossil fuels and releases the 'greenhouse' gas carbon dioxide along with other poisons. When finally 'uneconomic' to repair it is scrapped with waste and further pollution. These come in addition to the environmental impact of roads and the costs of accidents.

Marketing encourages the use of cars and many other hidden costs not paid for by the producer or the consumer. Packaging of consumer goods is another source of waste. Some products need protection in transit and display, but most packaging is designed to encourage a purchase.

Marketing can encourage people to buy more and more goods, many of which they hardly knew they needed. This places an ever-growing burden on natural resources and the environment.

 Packaging, page 48

Marketing encourages increasing consumption

It is argued that marketing has invaded our way of life. Advertisements, brand names and logos are found everywhere: in the street, on TV, in magazines, at sports events, concerts and art exhibitions – even on our clothes. From earliest childhood people are deluged with demands that they buy an endless stream of goods and services. Does marketing arouse 'false needs' which would never otherwise have been expressed? Does advertising inflame the greed in human nature and suggest that happiness depends on spending money?

There are no 'correct' answers to these questions. They raise important issues and everyone will have their own point of view.

What are the constraints?

Firms and marketing departments in particular face real constraints on their behaviour. These may be as follows.

Legal

Over recent years a wide range of consumer protection measures have been introduced. These laws give responsibilities to the firm and rights to the consumer.

 Key legislation, page 68

Through voluntary codes of practice

Firms and industries often take their own steps to ensure good practice in marketing. The reputation of most companies is far more valuable than any gains from poor practice. A growing proportion of firms issue their own codes of ethical practice which are always more demanding than the law. Then member firms of trade organisations from various industries often agree to observe rules for fair practice. Examples include the Association of British Travel Agents and the Federation of Master Builders.

The Advertising Standards Authority (ASA) is an independent organisation which was set up in 1962 to ensure that every advertisement is 'legal, decent, honest and truthful'. In addition advertisers must be socially responsible and their advertisements must be consistent with 'the principles of fair competition'. These requirements are set out in the ASA's Codes which apply to all non-broadcast media. TV advertising is regulated by the Independent Television Authority while advertisements on the radio are subject to the Radio Authority.

Through pressure groups

Organisations that put pressure on firms to behave more responsibly have increased in power and number. In most cases anyone is entitled to join and funds are obtained through subscriptions, merchandising and donations. Some pressure groups are very effective at gaining media interest in campaigns against certain companies. Greenpeace and Friends of the Earth are probably the best known groups but others campaign on such issues as animal rights, the dangers of smoking and the interests of small shareholders. Large firms with valuable brands are very sensitive to any publicity that might damage their reputation. This makes pressure groups surprisingly powerful.

ⒸASE STUDY

Shell v Greenpeace

Figure 3.34 *Greenpeace's occupation of the Brent Spar oil rig in 1995 gained considerable media interest*

In 1995 Shell announced plans to sink Brent Spar (an old oil storage rig) in the North Atlantic. Within months, Greenpeace had launched a high profile campaign against the oil company's decision. Battles followed between protesters and security staff as Greenpeace occupied the rig. The anti-Shell campaign was especially intense in Germany where consumers boycotted Shell petrol and some filling stations were fire-bombed. Shortly afterwards Shell backed down and announced that the rig would be broken up on land – at an extra cost of £36 million. Greenpeace later admitted to having used some misleading information while maintaining that its campaign had been right in principle.

Through consumer purchasing decisions

No product can remain in production unless it sells. Through their buying power consumers effectively 'vote' for or against products. If enough people refuse to buy a product that they consider unethical then the firm concerned will have to think again. Conversely, *adding* ethical qualities to a product may make good marketing sense. In the past decade many firms have tried to demonstrate that their products are environmentally friendly.

Appendix

Key Legislation

Consumer Protection Act (1987)

The Act makes provision for customers to take legal action against a supplier for injury caused by a defective product whether the product was sold to them or not and without having to prove the supplier was negligent. The Act also covers misleading price indications about goods, services or facilities available from a business.

Data Protection Acts (1984, 1998)

These Acts cover businesses, the self-employed and homeworkers who keep information, no matter how little, on computer about any living person. Almost any information other than a name, address and telephone number (with a few other exceptions) places an obligation to register with the Data Protection Registrar. Individuals have the right to see any computerised information held on them and to have incorrect information amended or deleted.

Once a business is registered, a Code of Practice is issued which requires the business to:

- keep the information secure
- ensure the information is accurate and relevant to its needs
- comply with individuals' right to see any computerised information held on them and to have incorrect information amended or deleted.

Sale of Goods Act (1979)

This Act is associated with the Supply of Goods and Services Act (1982), the Unfair Contract Terms Act (1977), the Supply of Goods (Implied Terms) Act (1973) and various EU directives.

The Act covers consumer rights when purchasing goods from a business. Goods must be as described, of merchantable quality and fit for their intended purpose. The Act also covers the conditions under which the customer can return goods.

Sunday Trading Act (1994)

If the floor area of the sales area is less than 280 square metres there are no restrictions on opening hours on Sunday; otherwise retailers can only open for six hours.

Supply of Goods and Services Act (1982)

This extends the protection for consumers provided by the Sale of Goods Act (1979) to services. The person or business providing the service must do so:

- for a reasonable charge
- within a reasonable time
- with reasonable care and skill.

Trade Descriptions Acts (1968, 1972)

These Acts prohibit the use of false descriptions of goods and services provided by a business. For any retailer the provisions apply where the description is given by another person (such as the manufacturer) and then repeated to the client or customer.

Index